REVIEWS FOR ANIMATION 101

"Ernest Pintoff's *Animation* 101 provides the reader with the underpinnings of a complex and multi-faceted animation world in an understandable and lively way. Clearly, Pintoff's text is destined t̶̶̶̶ ̶̶̶̶ ̶̶̶̶ ̶̶̶̶ Cal Arts students."

— Frank Te̶̶̶
Director,
California Institute of the Arts

"*Animation* 101 is a fascinating tour of the art's rich history and personal impact as seen through the eyes of animation professionals. Ernie Pintoff provides a renaissance introduction to a continually captivating species of moving images."

— Richard Weinberg, Ph.D.
Director, Computer Animation Laboratory
USC School of Cinema-Television

"Ernest Pintoff's book is as rich as animation, and as eclectic as the brilliant career of its author. He draws not only from his remarkable experience, but includes contributions from 20 widely different personalities. The result is entertaining, unexpected and enlightening."

— Michael Ocelot, President of ASIFA,
International Animated Film Association

"The words in *Animation* 101 come from someone who both loves the art and has contributed to it. I earnestly suggest that those really interested in entering the field read this book... In fact, read it twice."

— Joseph R. Barbera
Co-Chairman, Co-Founder
Hanna-Barbera Productions

ANIMATION 101

BY

ERNEST PINTOFF

OSCAR® WINNER FOR BEST ANIMATED SHORT, "THE CRITIC"

Published by Michael Wiese Productions, 11288 Ventura Blvd., Suite 821, Studio City, CA 91604, (818) 379-8799 Fax (818) 986-3408.
E-mail: wiese@earthlink.net
http://www.mwp.com

Cover design, photograph and illustrations by The Art Hotel
Interior design and layout by Gina Mansfield

Printed by McNaughton & Gunn, Inc., Saline, Michigan
Manufactured in the United States of America

The publisher plants two trees for every tree used in the manufacturing of this book. Printed on recycled stock.

Library of Congress Cataloging in Publication Data

Pintoff, Ernest,
        Animation 101/ by Ernest Pintoff,
          p.   cm.
        Includes bibliographical references (p.),
        ISBN: 0-941188-68-X
        1. Animation (Cinematography)   I. Title.
TR897.5.P56   1998
778.5'347--dc21   98-11981
                                                                                  CIP

ANIMATION 101
BY ERNEST PINTOFF

TABLE OF CONTENTS

PREFACE
by
Ernest Pintoff

Besides creating, writing and executing graphics, the most enriching aspect of my career has been animation teaching.

The intention of this book is to present an overview of animation past and present from an insider's point of view, featuring a variety of voices and perspectives. The book is for all of those who love animation and want to learn more about both its history and direction from professionals who share your enthusiasm. It is relevant to animation students as well as others interested in this exciting medium.

As a graduate student, I received an MFA in Art History. At the time, art was my passion. Now I wish I had pursued a broader liberal arts education, concentrating especially on literature, history and the social sciences. Walt Disney said, "An animator is best equipped if he is well-read. He should study the classics for construction, design and characterization, as well as for dramatic content." A career in animation could be extremely rewarding, both creatively and financially. Getting the right foundation is half the battle.

My own hands-on introduction in animation began as an apprentice *in-betweener* at the Walt Disney Studios, followed by my experience at United Productions of America, or UPA, in California. There, I was soon promoted to designer, then writer/director. As I was surrounded by consummate animation professionals, this proved to be an invaluable experience.

In 1955, I founded my own studio in New York City, which I called Pintoff Productions. There, I directed and produced animated and live-action commercials as well as short films and theatrical movies.

Animation 101 is written in the hope that my filmmaking experience might enable me to present animation enthusiasts with both a historical and personal overview of this fascinating art form. My course, *Animation 101*, was originally created as a primer for liberal arts and film students in both undergraduate and graduate programs. As such, the contents herein include some of my animation teaching experiences at the University of Southern California, the American Film Institute, Cal Arts in Valencia and the University of California in Los Angeles.

We shall cover the birth of American animation by discussing and celebrating the work of some of the major animation studios and seminal figures of the 20th century from Disney to Bakshi. To provide an in-depth look at this subject, as well as to cover all of the exciting figures of experimental animation both in the Americas and abroad, are beyond the scope of this primer. The encyclopedic Cartoons by Giannalberto Bendazzi is recommended for further reading.

To offer multiple perspectives, I have invited a number of renowned professionals to express their views. It is amazing how many back-grounds, techniques, and points of view are represented here. What comes through each essay, though, is a pure love of this beautiful form. I hope you have as much fun reading these articles as I had putting them together, and that these gleanings will inspire those of you who plan to do your own work in this field.

Looking back, I can say that it was my dad, a frustrated artist and musician, who was most influential in developing my own interest and passion regarding animation.

A hard-working shopkeeper and an affectionate father who loved music, he encouraged both my brother and me to play musical instruments. Frequently, my father told us about our family roots in Poland and Latvia, recounting stories about his early adventures in America. As a special treat, he would sometimes take us to the movies.

We were hugely impressed when he took us to see *Snow White and the Seven Dwarfs*. It was from that day on that I began to notice the names of the artists and animators on the credits rolling by, as I dreamed of emulating them one day.

ACKNOWLEDGMENTS

I would like to thank my colleagues as well as students who have contributed to this book. I am especially grateful to Pat Richards for her fine research and editing. Alan Berger and Joseph Manduke have been of valuable assistance, as were Jules Engel and Herbert Klynn for their ideas and advice.

Finally, I am most appreciative to my wife, Caroline, for her support, affection and numerous contributions.

Usually, a renowned filmmaker introduces a book such as this to readers. In this case, however, I asked Maureen Furniss, the distinguished animation writer, teacher, and publisher of *Animation Journal*, to write and share her enthusiasm about this remarkable art form.

FOREWORD
by
Maureen Furniss, Ph.D.

There are many interesting personalities in the field of animation, which is part of the reason I was drawn to it in the first place. Certainly Ernest Pintoff is one of them. His eclectic career includes work as a graphic artist, composer, writer, and animator, as well as a producer and director of animated and live-action advertisements, shorts, and features. However, I first saw Ernest in a different setting entirely. I met him when I visited the animation class he taught at the University of Southern California. And it seems that this role, more than any other, has continued to be foremost in my mind.

From reading this manuscript, I think the reader will recognize the breadth of Pintoff's background. Teaching has played an important part in his career, and now others may learn from his broad experience in the animation field. An artist and businessman, Pintoff's lessons address both the aesthetic and practical issues newcomers need to know. Certainly, I am one of the many people who have benefited greatly from his knowledge.

If you are considering a career in animation, this is a propitious time to enter the field. With the advent of cable and video markets as well as new techniques such as computer graphics, more animation than ever before is being created, and for all age groups. Along with this opening up, barriers of many kinds are being broken down; old constraints of gender, race, and the need for certain studio affiliations are disappearing now, so that many more people are able to find satisfying careers in animation. This diversity brings a greater range of content and formal expression to the field, so that all kinds of wonderful work is finding its way into distribution.

Now that I am a teacher myself, I am pleased to know that my students will be able to find opportunities for greater creative expression than they would have enjoyed even ten or fifteen years ago. It is not that fulfilling jobs are all that easy to come by, but they certainly do exist. Many people want these jobs, and often I get calls asking about the best way to break into animation.

First of all, you should explore your artistic capabilities in depth. Devote yourself to your artwork and create images constantly to bring out the full scope of your personal talents and aesthetic sensibilities. Think about the many fulfilling jobs that one can have within the industry, such as background painter, layout artist, colorist, or perhaps model builder, and see which best suits your special abilities. The actual job of animator encompasses only one relatively narrow aspect of the process. You should create a bulging life drawing portfolio before you ever go out on an interview. Of course, background artists also need to show examples of landscapes or other suitable artwork, while model builders need evidence of ability to create three-dimensional art, and so forth.

Secondly, make an effort to widen your circle of professional acquaintances. It does no good to meet the people you admire in a superficial way. Rather, join organizations and meet professionals through social events or by working with them on various projects. Also consider interviewing people for class projects--a professional attitude can help you develop a lasting friendship and get your foot in the door when it comes time for graduation.

Finally, I suggest that you go back into history. Explore those professionals who preceded you. Read a lot--this book makes a good start--and view a wide variety of works. Try not to limit yourself to the all-time favorites, but look into animation made across the world from the silent period to the present day. Finally, consider attending a large animation festival, where you can view contemporary work as well as historical retrospectives, plus meet professionals in the field. And good luck to you.

SOME PERSONAL FAVORITES

Traditionally, animation in this country has been produced for children. However, it is becoming apparent that a variety of categories with many viewers exist, such as family, young adult and mature audiences, just as they do for live action films.

I screen a variety of noteworthy animated features for my students, usually studying the works of various Disney animators in perennials such as *Snow White and the Seven Dwarfs*, *Pinocchio*, or *The Lion King*, as well as Halas and Batchelor's work on *Animal Farm*, George Dunning's direction and Heinz Edelman's design on *Yellow Submarine*, and Richard Williams' animation direction on *Who Framed Roger Rabbit?*

In choosing which animated shorts to screen, there is a wealth of talent to choose from, along with a great variety of styles. Animated shorts I often screen and especially recommend are some of the delightful *Betty Boop* films by Max Fleischer, UPA's The *Tell-tale Heart*, with Ted Parmelee's rendering of the Poe short story, UPA's *Unicorn in the Garden*, which is Bill Hurtz's surrealist adaptation of Thurber's story and line drawings, *Neighbors* by Norman McLaren, *The Hand* by Jiri Trnka, John Hubley's *The Line* (with voice-over characterizations by Dizzy Gillespie and Dudley Moore), *The Nose* by Alexandre Alexieff, Jan Lenica's *Rhinoceros*, from the Eugene Ionesco play, *Binery Bits* by John Whitney, one of Mike Judge's "Beavis and Butthead" episodes, and *Tin Toy* by John Lasseter.

There are many outstanding graphic designers, but several stand out. Maurice Binder designed the arresting, dramatic title sequences for many James Bond films. The evocative work of Saul Bass is legendary. Besides conceiving and animating the main title and credits for such varied works as *The Man With The Golden Arm*, *West Side Story*,

GoodFellas and *The Age of Innocence*, he received an Academy Award for one of his own live-action short subjects, entitled *Why Man Creates*. After designing the title sequence to Hitchcock's masterpiece, *Vertigo*, he was hired by Hitchcock to not only design the title sequences of *North by Northwest* and *Psycho*, but to serve as visual consultant on those films. Pablo Ferro, who designed and executed the title sequences for *Dr. Strangelove*, *Clockwork Orange*, *As Good As It Gets*, and *L.A. Confidential*, among many others, developed the use of single projected multiple screens.

FROM DISNEY TO BAKSHI

Born in Chicago in 1901 of an Irish-Canadian family, Walt Disney had a difficult childhood, filled with severe privations. He received protection from his elder brother Roy, which continued in the form of financial backing in their adult life. His father, an itinerant ne'er-do-well, moved his family from Chicago to Missouri to Kansas City. The Disney boys began working when still young children. An escape from this rather nightmarish reality was drawing, which became young Walt's passion. What he did willingly carry from his youth was a love of the American countryside. It was the pastoral life of rural Missouri that provided the best memories for the adult Disney, and lovingly-depicted country scenes, with winding roads and birds twittering on the trees, are a Disney trademark.

Disney managed to take a class at the Kansas City Art Institute in his early teens. After volunteering for the Red Cross in 1918 after a final disagreement with his father, he worked in France as an ambulance driver just as World War I was ending. Entertaining the other soldiers with his caricatures, he was encouraged to try his hand at either comic strips or graphic art. Back in Kansas City, he landed a job producing animated commercials for local movie theatres. It was there, in 1919, that he met another animator, the gifted Ub Iwerks. They became fast friends. After a short while Disney decided to form his own small company, continuing to produce animated commercials, then in 1922 going on to make his own theatrical cartoon shorts.

While Iwerks had the better talent for cartooning, Disney possessed great imagination, organizational ability, and drive. Together they assembled other animators to form a small, talented team, including Hugh Harman, Rudolf Ising, and Carmen "Max" Maxwell. However, almost immediately the Disney and Iwerks firm went bankrupt, partly because his distributors folded, and partly as a result of Disney's deep unwillingness to stint on quality. Even these earliest films are notable for an unusual degree of background detail, especially for that period, with the use of a full range of wash tones and other luxuries.

So it was that in 1923, undaunted, he took a train to Los Angeles with his brother Roy, ever his financial backer and manager. They set about renting a small studio in Hollywood, and then one at a time, Disney sent for Iwerks and his other Kansas City colleagues. He then produced a successful series of shorts. His first, blending live action and animation, was entitled *Alice in Cartoonland*. Next, collaborating with distributors Charles Mintz and George Winkler, Disney originated a series entitled *Oswald The Lucky Rabbit*, which was even more well received in the trade press. After his distributors threatened to take the characters and many of his key animators away from him, a shocked Disney vowed never to relinquish ownership of his creations again.

Undeterred by this unforeseen setback, Disney thought up a new character called Mickey Mouse.

The first two Mickey Mouse films, *Plane Crazy* and *Gallopin' Gaucho*, were silent, but the third one, entitled *Steamboat Willie*, had dialogue, and the music exactly fit the action. Released in 1928, this short became an immediate hit. The Walt Disney name was firmly established in Hollywood, and his reputation had become that of a creative and financial risk-taker who continuously reinvested his profits back into the business. It is interesting to note here that Disney did all the

Steamboat Willie

© Disney Enterprises, Inc.

voice-overs as Mickey Mouse from *Steamboat Willie* in 1928 to *Fun And Fancy Free* in 1946.

Although many projects were not immediately profitable, the Walt Disney Studio has made millions of dollars with box-office bonanzas, beginning with the first full-length animated feature ever produced, *Snow White and the Seven Dwarfs*. This 1937 film combined a degree of seriousness and artistry which were unheard of in animation. Disney was reportedly so nervous at the premiere that he couldn't sit through the film, instead pacing outside, now wondering if the audience was laughing with him or at him, now wondering if an adult audience could possibly be dramatically stirred by his animated offering. He need not have worried. Disney became the most successful producer

Snow White and the Seven Dwarfs

© *Disney Enterprises, Inc.*

in the history of filmmaking, and his studio's early groundbreaking work is responsible for most of the standard animation techniques used today.

In the early 1960s, "Uncle Walt" became a friend to little children all over America, as his paternal countenance appeared on the small screen each Sunday evening. With his kindly voice, he spoke directly into the camera to introduce each episode of "The Wonderful World of Disney," which featured live action stories or animated adventures for children. Around the same time, Disney was able to realize a long-cherished dream by developing Disneyland in Anaheim, California.

Perhaps due to his own harsh childhood, he was impelled to create a world designed especially for children. Later, Disneyworld in Florida was built. Most recently, Disney has developed Euro Disney in Paris as well as resorts and theme parks in Japan.

Yet Disney himself was never a wealthy man, having been forced, for example, to borrow against his own life insurance to help finance Disneyland. It was his perfectionism as well as his ambitious enterprises which kept the company in a constant state of indebtedness, and his tolerant brother Roy in a constant state of alarm, right up until Walt's death in 1966, when a more conservative management team assumed control. The acquisition of money did not seem to mean much to Disney; he rather cheerfully used it up to build his dreams.

When asked to recount a final anecdote on Mr. Disney, many animators mention his ability to inspire his staff. "He had a talent to draw out of guys what they didn't have," stated studio veteran Frank Thomas. Part of that inspiration came from his amazing storytelling skills. When commencing a project, he would gather his animators together much like children and vividly recount to them the story they were about to work on, using a variety of entertaining voice changes, body movements, and so on. It was as if the stories really did come to life in Disney's febrile imagination. He was the kind of grown-up who could unabashedly build a giant toy train in his backyard, which he then enjoyed with his own children. After his own dark childhood, it is his genius for both feeling and conveying a child's delight that is Walt Disney's most enduring legacy.

Now, a word on the famous and influential people at Warner Brothers. At first, the studio began by imitating Disney, which was the dominant force in 1930s animation. However, by the mid-1930s, Warner Brothers animation found its own way, developing a distinctive brash humor which is still fresh and truly funny today. Instead of trying to compete with Disney in the field of full-length feature animation, they wisely concentrated on the animated short, which suited their zany humor best. Ex-Disney animators Hugh Harman, Rudolf Ising, and Isadore "Friz" Freleng started the studio in the late 1920s. They were able to attract a visionary producer, Leon Schlesinger, then chief of Pacific Art and Title, who had connections at Warner Brothers. In 1930, Harman and Ising began their wildly successful Looney Tunes series. After they left, outstanding talent such as Chuck Jones, Tex Avery, Bob Clampett, Bobe Cannon, Friz Freleng and Frank Tashlin propelled the animation studio forward. These sublimely talented

Chuck Jones

and rebellious animators created immortal cartoon characters like Daffy Duck, Bugs Bunny, Porky Pig, The Road Runner, Wile E. Coyote, Tweety, Sylvester, and many more.

As for MGM, they began by utilizing outside contractors for animation productions. From 1930 to 1934, Ub Iwerks supplied animated short subjects to the studio. Afterwards, it was Harman and Ising who launched the Happy Harmonies series. But MGM was not happy about the high costs of Harman and Ising's work, and in 1937 started its own cartoon studio. In 1940, the studio launched the *Tom and Jerry* series, created by two young in-house animators, William Hanna and Joseph Barbera. They worked well as a team, with Barbera writing the stories, making sketches and inventing gags, while Hanna provided the direction.

After Harman and Ising left the studio in the early 1940s, MGM was able to snag the great Tex Avery, master of the gag cartoon. Meanwhile, the team of Bill Hanna and Joe Barbera went on to win five Academy Awards with the wildly successful *Tom and Jerry* films for MGM.

In 1944, Gene Kelly realized his dream of doing a dance with a cartoon character by teaming with Hanna and Barbera to create the intricate and impressive *Anchors Aweigh*.

Tex Avery continued to create a constant stream of hilarious material at MGM through the early 1950s, when he left for a well-deserved sabbatical. In 1947, he created what many considered his comic masterpiece, *King Size Canary*.

In 1954, MGM released its first wide-screen cartoon. But MGM decided to close its cartoon studio in the spring of 1957, and it was then that the Hanna-Barbera team really took off.

It was in 1957 that William Hanna and Joseph Barbera launched their very own production company, a natural extension of years of working together tightly as an effective team. Together they created numerous popular series for television. Among their shows are "The Flintstones," "Huckleberry Hound," "Ruff and Reddy" and "Quick Draw McGraw." In addition, the team produced *The Flintstones*, their first live-action feature.

From the beginning of their corporate partnership, Hanna-Barbera rescued the floundering animation industry by offering more employment for artists, writers and technicians than any other studio had since Walt Disney in the 1930s. Ironically, bowing to television's economic pressures, Hanna-Barbera stripped the medium of animation to its barest essentials and removed much of the art.

Because of Hanna-Barbera's television work, they are probably the best known animators in the world, having produced over twenty-five thousand feet of film a week for television alone. All of Hanna-Barbera's cartoon characters have been extremely well-merchandised.

The various anatomical positions of Hanna-Barbera animated characters have become standardized and as a result, their *model sheets* include every movement, even indicating looks of shock, and every character's entry and exit. To produce a new sequence, it is sufficient for an animator to simply draft a *storyboard*, then feed it into a computer for the ability to generate *computer generated* animation. Animators no longer have to sketch repetitive movements, but they merely make lists of numbers already stored in a computer's memory. This technique has been used successfully with the likes of "Rod Rocket," "Space Ghost," "Crusader Rabbit," "King Leonardo" and "Deputy Dawg."

At the other end of the spectrum, let us say a word about one of the more dissident voices to reach success in the field of commercial animation. In 1938, a highly original cartoonist named Ralph Bakshi was born and raised in Brooklyn. In trouble as a teenager, he was encouraged to develop his evident drawing skills by a social worker. And he went on to bring his tough street sensibility to his best films.

Hired at the age of eighteen as an *opaquer* by Gene Deitch, the Terrytoons studio new creative head, Bakshi became an animator in his early twenties and soon became a full-fledged director, piloting cartoons such as "Deputy Dawg" and theatrical shorts such as *James Hound*. In 1966, Bakshi was appointed supervising director of the Terrytoons studio and created an imaginative television series called, "The Mighty Heroes."

Shortly thereafter, Bakshi left Terrytoons to run Paramount Pictures' New York based studio which was still producing animated shorts for theatrical release. Before the year was out, however, Gulf and Western decided to close the Paramount Pictures animation division. Shortly thereafter, Bakshi and producer Steve Krantz put together a low-budget feature entitled *Fritz The Cat*, which was originally created by outrageous Underground comics legend Robert Crumb. Touted as "the first X-rated animated cartoon," *Fritz The Cat* made waves as well as money by being a sexy and vibrant satire. In 1973, *Heavy Traffic* was even more impressive. It was an explosive and intense semi-autobiographical street saga set in New York City.

That feature used a revolutionary combination of live-action and animation techniques.

Bakshi's third feature, a scathing social satire called *Coonskin* proved to be too controversial, as it harshly depicted the hell-on-earth of the New York ghetto and satirized Blacks, Jews and Italians. It was shelved by Paramount Pictures after igniting a firestorm of protest at its first showings.

Along with producer Martin Rosen, Bakshi turned to the safer territory of science fiction for *Wizards* in 1977 and attempted to film at least part of J.R.R. Tolken's *Lord Of The Rings*. But animation fans were distressed to learn that Bakshi had *rotoscoped* the animated movements from live-action figures. That technique was also used in the 1981 feature, called, *American Pop*, which traced the evolution of 20th century music in America.

Bakshi's career moved in fits and starts after that and with box-office failures impeding some of his more ambitious plans, he spent most of his time painting.

Resurfacing in 1987 as producer of a new "Mighty Mouse" series for television, Bakshi returned to his Terrytoons roots, but this time with a new slant, since the actual dialogue of the show was left to his protégé, John Kricfalusi. The two collaborated on an animated music video for Mick Jagger called *Harlem Shuffle*. Having previously blended live-action and animation, Bakshi revived the idea in 1992 for *Cool World*, his first feature film in many years.

In the mid-nineties, Bakshi made a controversial animated television series for HBO called "Spicy City," that featured sexy and seedy characters.

THE ANIMATION PROCESS

In as much as my course is designed for students interested in animation but not necessarily in becoming animators, I spend a brief time discussing the how-to aspects of animation.

Storyboarding is the conceptual planning often used in all kinds of filmmaking. It is the visual system for making a detailed analysis of the film's development, including character appéarance and movement, detailed work-up of backgrounds, delineation of scenes and sequences, and notes on music and sound effects. Illustrated storyboards were originally created because the visual concept may have been easier to draw than to write. Conceptualization is the essential function of the storyboard, and getting it down on paper is the vital first step.

Some questions that the act of storyboarding will help clarify are: Is the information clearly presented? Are the characters clearly and sharply conceived? Is the story clear? Is the idea effectively presented?

Commercial animation production houses and advertising agencies have developed storyboarding into a special art form. The renderings are made by artists who paste each drawing onto a pre-cut mounting board. A typical storyboard will also contain dialogue and action not depicted in the renderings. The process of visual thinking usually releases new energy and new ideas. No less important, a storyboard enables one to see all the problems.

There are many types of animation with which one might experiment. Paper cutout animation involves moving figures that have been drawn on a piece of paper and then cut out. The force of gravity and a glass pressure plate or platen, with registration pins, holds these figures flat against the background scene. The animator's own hand moves the cutout pieces across the scene. Positioned overhead, the animation camera clicks off one, two, three, or sometimes four exposures between each movement. The most renowned early film of this genre is Lotte Reiniger's 1926 feature, *The Adventures of Prince Achmed*, which she completed when still in her twenties. In 1964, Guilio Gianini and Emmanuele Luzzati made a superb cutout film entitled *The Thieving Magpie*, based on Rossini's opera. Many more independent animation artists have experimented successfully with this medium.

Generally, such animation is probably best for stories or plots featuring lots of physical action. Conversely, it is difficult to deal effectively with story nuances as revealed through more detailed movement, figures, facial expressions and backgrounds. For instance, if you have a story in which a character becomes angry, the character would likely need to express that fury. As with all kinds of animation, limits are connected with the technique and materials that are employed.

Animation of three-dimensional objects, such as geometric shapes and forms, has long fascinated filmmakers and audiences. Stories tend to be more concrete and simpler with this technique than with character animation.

The ultimate refinement of three-dimensional animation is probably best represented by puppet animation techniques that have been originated and refined in Eastern Europe. Renowned artists in this area include George Pal, Ladislas Starevitch, Hermina Tyrlova, Zenon Wasilewski, Karel Zeman, Jiri Trnka, Jan Lenica, and Bretislav Pojar. The basic principles of single-frame movement and photography apply here. Animation puppets themselves are built to be sturdy, freestanding, with movable body joints, well executed, and able to be viewed from 360 degrees. The puppet's anatomy begins with an armature, an inner construction that allows the puppet to be both sturdy and flexible. It is useful to note that puppet animation techniques require the creation of an entire new world. The animator must build mini-sets appropriate for the story, keeping in mind elements of scale, stability, camera access and dramatic lighting.

Few animation techniques more fully exploit the medium's power than claymation or clay animation. Here, a three-dimensional piece of clay is moved incrementally, and can transform itself through countless variations. In shooting clay animation, the camera is mounted horizontally and stage lighting is sometimes required. Eli Noyes was one of the first to use clay animation. Today, British animation artist Nick Park is an innovator in this medium.

Of course, most popular among traditional animation techniques is cel animation, which involves bringing drawings to life. The term "cel" is derived from the transparent sheets of celluloid used and developed by Walt Disney, Ub Iwerks, Max Fleisher, and Walter Lantz.

The use of such cels enables one to change a component within a scene without again drawing every single element. The transparent surface of a plastic sheet makes it easier to attain more detailed and finely rendered results than if every element of the drawing has to be re-drawn each time a change is required. The standard animation cel is .005 of an inch thick, measures 10 1/2 by 13 inches, and is usually punched to fit a #12 field that accommodates one of two standard registration systems, either Oxberry or Acme.

Once the cels and backgrounds have been completed, they are placed on a vertically mounted animation stand and photographed.

Full-cel animation requires *exposure sheets*, also known as *bar sheets*. This is a system for recording the sequence and order of the various cel layers, the number of exposures given to those layers, and to the movements of the camera.

As for the actual working team, the animation producer is the individual in charge of the nuts and bolts of making the film, making sure that it comes in on time and on budget. The animation writer often creates the subject, defines the characters, and begins shaping the story line and dialogue. The storyboard artist breaks the story down into component scenes. Once the track is analyzed, the timing is worked out by the lead animator. Then, it is fine-tuned by the director. Meanwhile, background artists render each background needed for the film.

Usually, different animators are assigned to draw different scenes or characters, unless the film is very short. Directors create extremes, or maximum action points, for the drawings that are necessary for the film. These are drawn roughly on paper sheets. The assistant animators execute the *in-betweens*. Then the completed paper drawings may be filmed in a pencil test. Next, the drawings are converted to cel by computer. The checker makes sure that everything is properly executed and identified. Finally, a camera operator, or team of operators, photographs the cels. The film editor cuts together pieces of exposed film and matches images to the sound track.

Essentially, the editor works with the sound crew, voice-over actors, composers and musicians in recording the sound track for the finished movie. Sound effects may also be indicated on the bar sheets and added in the final editing or mixing process.

One can understand why producers like shortcuts. Shortcuts allow them to make the longest film using the least amount of labor, which of course, saves money. Hence, limited-cel animation.

Faith and John Hubley

14

In the sixties, John and Faith Hubley created simple but artfully designed animated shorts. However, their high standards have not been adopted by the rather static Saturday morning fare on American television today.

In planning their films, directors of traditional limited-cel productions try to limit or hold certain cels wherever possible. Characteristic of limited animation are endless camera pans over static backgrounds. In order to recycle drawings from program to program, silhouette chases are employed and scenes are consistently drawn from an identical perspective.

Many students are fascinated by computer animation, and rightly so. The rapid development of computer graphics, simulation and computer animation in the past twenty years has been breathtaking.

In 1981, John Halas became one of the first traditional animators to work in this medium with his short film *Dilemma* at Computer Creations. Then, the Disney Studios experimented with *Where the Wild Things Are*, which blended cel animation with computer animation. Subsequently, John Lasseter went on to do innovative work in the field of computer animation. Then, Susan Van Baerle's *Snoot and Muttly* and Lucasfilm's *The Adventures of Andre and Wally B* (designed by Lasseter) began making the rounds of animation festivals and won numerous awards.

As the 1980s progressed, stellar films continued to make waves in this new medium. Disney's 1982 experimental full-length offering, *Tron*, was a computer-animated and live-action hybrid with a lukewarm story line but stunning special effects. Then, Chris Wedge produced the much-noticed *Tuber's Two Step*, and John Lasseter, now at Pixar, produced both *Luxo Jr.* and *Tin Toy*, the latter being the first computer animated film to win an Oscar. In 1995, with Pixar's delightful *Toy Story*, the computer animated feature film had come of age.

Throughout the 1990s, smaller and less expensive computer systems have opened the creative channels to many artists. This new accessibility has been vital to computer animation's growth. And happily, animators around the world are putting much creative input into the development of this new medium.

CLASSIC VOICE-OVER ARTISTS

Perhaps the most talented voice-over actor ever was Mel Blanc. This comedy genius created the character voices of numerous Warner Bros. cartoon characters, including Bugs Bunny, Daffy Duck, Porky Pig, Tweety, Sylvester, Yosemite Sam, Foghorn Leghorn and Pepe Le Pew.

Blanc also performed voice-overs for MGM and Warner Bros. as well as for Columbia Pictures and other major studios. In later years, he was equally busy on television as Barney Rubble in "The Flintstones." In the early 1950s, Blanc was associated with the beloved American comic Jack Benny and although his live-action movie appearances were not extensive, Blanc and his zany characters enjoyed engaging moments in movies such as *Neptune's Daughter* and *Champagne For Caesar*, before taking time off in 1988 to write his autobiography, entitled, *That's Not All, Folks!*.

Back in 1945, a young comic actor named Stan Freberg was looking for work in Hollywood. As a young actor trying to break into show business, Freberg would often take the bus from his home in Pasadena to downtown Hollywood, "read" for producers, then ride back to Pasadena. Finally, his agent arranged an audition for the inexperienced comic at Warner Bros. cartoons.

At a mike behind the curtain in the projection room, Freberg went through a series of voices and impersonations, including FDR, Jimmy Durante, Peter Lorre and Edward R. Murrow. Seated in the audience were Chuck Jones, Friz Freleng and Bob Clampett. Obviously, the animators there liked what they heard because they applauded enthusiastically. Friz Freleng finally approached Freberg excitedly and asked, "Why haven't we heard of you before, kid?"

Three days later at Warner Bros., with a new Screen Actors Guild card in his pocket, Freberg found himself alongside the legendary Mel Blanc.

Over the years, Freberg worked with such animators as Chuck Jones and Friz Freleng, who hired him to do the voice-over for a puppy named Chester.

Freberg also sang a hip version of "The Three Little Pigs" for Friz Freleng in *The Three Little Bops*. Later, Freberg performed voice-overs for several Warner Bros. animation directors and also worked for Tex Avery, George Pal, Walter Lantz, Hanna-Barbera and The Walt Disney Studios.

Stan Freberg

In addition to doing the voice-over for a beaver in Disney's *Lady and the Tramp*, Freberg also provided the voice-overs for several UPA cartoons in the late 1950s.

In addition to Freberg's stint as a commercial producer and syndicated commentator on radio, he provided voice-overs on several animated series such as "Tiny Toons" and "Garfield."

Over the years, Freberg has enjoyed a cult following throughout the world. "Animation is the perfect medium for comedy," he says. "Animated characters can move a helluva lot faster than live ones, and so can the jokes!"

Freberg believes that the whole process of working in this field--working with artists and animation directors, along with comic actors, waiting for *pencil tests*, then seeing the completed animation, will always be a pure joy.

18

Yet another classic voice-over talent is actor Chuck McCann, who created voices for puppets and cartoons as well as acting and producing animation since the age of twelve.

Growing up in New York City, McCann was lucky to have a father who was the musical arranger at the Roxy Theatre, so every afternoon after school, he was permitted to sit in the balcony and watch the short films of Laurel and Hardy, Buster Keaton, Charlie Chaplin, Bugs Bunny, Daffy Duck, and Porky Pig.

The Warner Bros. cartoons stood out for young McCann, particularly because of the comic genius of Mel Blanc, along with the short films of Friz Freleng and Chuck Jones. Other acting as well as comedic voice-over influences in McCann's career were Daws Butler, Stan Freberg and Paul Frees. In 1968, McCann was featured as a compelling live-action character in *The Heart Is A Lonely Hunter*, adapted from Carson McCullers' poignant novel.

Because of his uncanny ability to impersonate stars from film and television, McCann remains active in live-action dubbing, in addition to creating and performing numerous voice-over animation characterizations.

The new animation tools which we now possess, McCann says, can take us to exciting horizons, providing we observe the words of William Shakespeare, "The play's the thing!"

Among the many outstanding female voice-over artists is Mae Questel, who gave voice to both Betty Boop and Olive Oyl. Another is June Foray, who, among many characterizations, did the voice-overs for both Rocky and Natasha on the "Rocky and Bullwinkle" show. Pat Carroll and Patti Deutsch are well-known for their voice-over work in

Betty Boop

19

numerous commercials. A good current example of a traditional comic actress finding a voice-over niche is that of Julie Kavner; who gives a distinctive raspy voice to Marge in the hit prime-time cartoon, "The Simpsons."

Julie Kavner

A BRIEF HISTORY OF MUSIC AND SOUND

Music and sound effects are especially vital to animated tales, and have been used throughout animation's history to great comic and dramatic effect.

Back in the mid 1930s, a favorite American theatre experience involved the projection of slides and lyrics to well-known tunes, and this became routine even before movies were popular. A live singer or musician would invite the audience to sing along. Later, film producers adopted this idea, either transferring the slides to motion picture film or illustrating lyrics with drawings and live-action footage.

Max Fleischer was first to bring movement to what had previously been a static presentation by combining traditional sing-along featurettes with humor and invention. Those animated cartoons created a unique interactive bond between the film and its audience, which became a two-way communication, transcending the traditional active-passive roles of performer and viewer in a lively way.

The early sing-along short films were framed by cartoons sequences with *Koko The Clown*, as a bouncing ball hit each syllable of the lyrics in time with the song. Often, a Fleischer employee pointed a stick with a luminescent tip with the animated ball in time with the music, right in the theatre.

Realizing immediately the value of music for his animation productions, Disney sent for an old acquaintance named Carl Stalling. Stalling played the organ accompaniment for silent pictures back in Kansas City. Not only had Stalling composed and arranged the music for *Steamboat Willie*, but when he joined Disney, he proposed the idea for *The Skeleton Dance* and launched the *Silly Symphony* animated movies.

The Skeleton Dance was a bold concept in many ways. First, it did not feature familiar characters. Second, it was neither a story nor a vehicle for sight gags and third, it was designed to conform to a specific music track. The completed film was a triumph for both Disney and Stalling. Although nearly sixty years have passed and countless changes have occurred in animation, *The Skeleton Dance* remains as one of the best short cartoons ever made.

Together, Disney and Stalling developed methods of collaboration which produced some of the most outstanding film scores of any studio. Stalling continued his success at Warner Bros, retiring as musical director in 1958. He was replaced by Milt Franklyn, the man who had been his arranger.

The enormous success of *The Jazz Singer* had set Hollywood ablaze over the commercial prospects of talking pictures. Studios and theatre owners were divided in their reaction to sound, but the voice of the public was clear. . . "Talkies meant big business!" While many producers debated the merits of converting to all-sound production, Disney saw it as an opportunity to provide something unique: A synchronized sound cartoon.

In the late 1920s, Max Fleisher announced the arrival of *Talkartoons*, something entirely different. For the first time, cartoons would be actual talking pictures, as opposed to short subjects which were synchronized after their creation.

In the 1930s, the task of integrating the music and providing the scores over at Terrytoons fell to Phil Scheib, a classically-trained European composer. When Gene Deitch, the former UPA animation director, took the helm at Terrytoons in 1958, he too brought along new musical concepts.

It should be noted that later UPA's chief music and sound editor Joe Siracusa was responsible for the studio's unique music and sound tracks, especially for *Gerald McBoing Boing* and *Mr. Magoo*. Siracusa was a musician, performing as a percussionist with the Cleveland Philharmonic Orchestra and playing with the outlandish Spike Jones and His City Slickers. UPA was instrumental in introducing jazz to their scores and hired Shorty Rogers to write the music for *The Three Little Bops*. Other jazz composers, such as by Buddy Collette, Chico Hamilton and Shelly Manne were also active at the innovative cartoon studio.

The Walt Disney opus of 1940, *Fantasia*, was an ambitious marriage of music and animation which remains a classic to this day. Also notable was its groundbreaking use of multichannel stereophonic sound. The scene of the tutu-clad hippos and pirouetting alligators were from Ponchielli's *Dance Of The Hours*. Perhaps the most memorable scene from the film is Mickey Mouse's disastrous turn as "The Sorcerer's Apprentice," with music of Paul Dukas. In addition, the music of Beethoven, Tchaikovsky, Stravinsky, Ponchinelli, Mussorgsky, and Shubert were used in the film.

Because of his penchant for originality, Disney's film scores stand out as distinct musical pieces in their own right. *Snow White and the Seven Dwarfs* for its melodic charm, and *Pinocchio* for its wit. Throughout the years, several original musical compositions from Disney animated features have won Academy Awards in the best song category. Among the most notable were songs from *Pinocchio* in 1941, *The Jungle Book* in 1967, *The Little Mermaid* in 1989 and *The Lion King* in 1994.

ANIMATION 101

Although this course emphasizes history over practical training, some classes do contain a good proportion of students with some animation background. In such cases, I emphasize how to develop concepts and writing for animation. Students present and "pitch," or sell, a story-board or script as though the class and I were decision-makers at a major film studio. After each presentation, I offer my criticism, then invite the class to comment on their colleague's work.

Although various aspects of animation are examined, special emphasis is placed on commitment and the student's choice of material. I suggest that students present a synopsis of their scene before or after their pitch.

I emphasize the importance of writing as well as "casting." It is essential to direct material only with which one is familiar. Mostly, I urge students to select material with which they have an emotional bond and connection.

One great advantage to studying in a major production city such as Los Angeles is the plethora of student internships made available at all of the major animation studios. This is an excellent way for students with some background to garner some practical experience and make professional contacts.

As for getting employment in the field of animation, a storyboard or sample reel which demonstrates one's work is what those in hiring positions primarily consider. An alternative would be to produce a modestly budgeted original animated short and personally arrange for its distribution. A list of international festivals is available from the *Academy Of Motion Picture Arts And Sciences*. Some of the competitions listed are also open to avant-garde or experimental films.

I very much enjoy showing a variety of experimental or independent short films in my class. Experimental animation may deal with movement, form, or light, as opposed to linear stories. One innovative pioneer of experimental films was Len Lye from New Zealand, who developed the technique of drawing or painting directly on film. Another experimental filmmaker from New York, named Carmen D'Avino, created a short entitled *Pianissimo*, in which animated shapes danced in *stop-motion* on an upright piano. In 1964, *Pianissimo* was nominated for an Oscar. Earlier, however, Lucky Strike Cigarettes used the stop-motion technique in the production of television commercials which depicted their cigarettes popping out of packets to the strains of "Lucky tastes good like a cigarette should."

I strongly recommend that my students interested in a career in animation learn about its business aspects.

It is apparent that the responsibilities of the animation creator and writer are interrelated. Their work is frequently compared to that of the conductor of an orchestra or the captain of a ship and the animation director is usually viewed as providing the guiding force. Ultimately, however, the outcome of a film is determined by the concept, with the director, writer, designer and producer providing the organizational structure.

I also show my students drawings from my animated short films, *The Violinist*, *The Interview*, *The Critic* and *The Old Man and the Flower*.

The Violinist

The Old Man and the Flower

Flebus

27

MY LIFE IN ANIMATION

My personal animation production experiences have been somewhat unorthodox.

After receiving my M.F.A. from Michigan State University in 1953 and lured by the glamour of show business, I ventured West with portfolio in hand. Without any previous animation knowledge or training, I was fortunate to be hired by UPA in Hollywood.

After rather bitter disputes concerning hours, wages and working conditions, a few key people had broken from the Walt Disney Studios and in 1945 established United Productions of America. Among the founders were artist/director Steve Bosustow, designer/director John Hubley, and writer/director Pete Burness. The formation of UPA was undoubtedly a rejuvenating factor in establishing significant new directions in the field of animation. Bosustow took on most of the studio's executive responsibilities, while the day to day running of production was left to Herbert Klynn. Jules Engel was the key graphics head, and it was the prolific Pete Burness who was largely responsible for the writing of the popular Mr. Magoo series. The character of Magoo was created by John Hubley, who drew from his uncle and W.C. Fields as the inspiration for the cartoon curmudgeon. Hubley went on to direct the first three animated shorts, including *Ragtime Bear*, which introduced Magoo.

Winning Academy Awards for *When Magoo Flew* in 1954 and for *Gerald McBoing Boing* in 1955 substantiated UPA's position as the predominant animation influence of the mid-sixties.

Mr. Magoo

© UPA

29

Fortunately, I had the opportunity to work with Jules Engel and to share an office with avant-garde filmmaker John Whitney, who became my

first mentor. Whitney and I co-directed "Aquarium," "Lion Hunt" and "Blues Pattern" for "The Gerald McBoing Boing Show," network television's first venture into original animation programming. The "Twirliger Twins" were also created for this show. Whitney, an animation pioneer, had already gained international recognition for his short film entitled, *Celery Stalks At Midnight* using a jazz track, which was innovative at the time. Having been a composer and jazz musician since high school, I was excited to work with composers such as Shorty

Gerald McBoing Boing

© UPA

Rogers, Shelly Manne and Chico Hamilton. Scores for animated films were now reaching in all directions.

Besides Whitney, my other mentor at UPA was Robert Cannon, who had animated several *Bugs Bunny* short films at Warner Bros. It was Cannon who taught me the importance of probing deeply for story originality.

© UPA

The Twirliger Twins

After one year on the West Coast, I moved back East and went to work for Terrytoons. There, I conceived and wrote a story about a funny-looking character for a theatrical animated short called *Flebus*.

Flebus resembled a UPA cartoon in visual style, point of view and format. Together with veteran Terrytoon animator, Jim Tyer, who resembled W.C. Fields, I was able to bring my film to life. As well as writing and directing, I composed the film's musical score. This was a breakthrough at Terrytoons, which until my arrival, had their musical director, Phil Shieb, write, conduct and supervise all the musical scores for their productions.

After *Flebus* won first prize as best animated short at the San Francisco Film Festival and the Brussels Worlds Fair, I decided to open my own company in New York City which I called Pintoff Productions. Our specialty was the production of animated commercials for advertising agencies. The awards garnered by *Flebus* helped get my first animation spot and I was off and running.

With a staff of animators which included Jim Murakami, Jim Hiltz, Jack Schnerk and Howard Beckerman, we created commercials for such companies as Ford, Tip Top Bread, Lucky Strike Cigarettes and Renault automobiles.

Enjoying the economic rewards that resulted from our work for ad agencies, and, inspired by Disney, I re-invested the profits from our company and soon began producing independent films. My animated short, *The Violinist*, was made in 1958, *The Interview* in 1959, and *The Old Man and the Flower* in 1960. *The Critic* was produced in 1962 and won the Academy Award.

Later that year, I decided to abandon the production of animated commercials and shorts to focus on writing, directing and producing live-action films. Subsequently, I wrote, directed and produced *The Shoes*, my first live-action movie in 16mm.

I approached several big companies to distribute my short films, but found they had little interest in them. When I screened *The Violinist* to Columbia Pictures executives, they turned it down cold, exclaiming that the film was "too simple!" Taking matters into my own hands, I promoted all my films independently, through screenings at various New York City movie theatres.

The Violinist was favorably reviewed by *New York Times* film critic, Bosley Crowther and drew special attention when it won the British Academy Award and was nominated for an Oscar. Not surprisingly, distributors changed their minds about *The Violinist* and eventually

Columbia Pictures became the sole distributor of both my animated and live-action films.

As with all of my animated shorts, elements of *The Violinist* soundtrack, including voice, sound effects and music, were pre-mixed so that the animation could be created to follow the action with frame-by-frame precision. This technique also allowed for speedy and economical production.

Carl Reiner, who had worked as a writer with Mel Brooks on "The Sid Caesar Show" was a key figure in *The Violinist*, by bringing his humor, wit and voice to that film.

It was Reiner who introduced Brooks to me and it was Brooks who created *The Critic's* concept. Mel told me that while watching an arty animated film in a Manhattan theatre, he overheard a man with a Yiddish accent muttering, 'What the hell am I paying two dollars for this junk?' Brooks was amused by the idea as well as I.

I found that I could identify with the concept because of my own experiences as a modern painter. At that time I was experimenting with my own non-objective paintings and wanted to poke fun at the bewildered reactions that people had with my work, often remarking, "What the hell is that, Pintoff?"

As the graphic basis for *The Critic*, I asked our studio cameraman, Bob Heath, to shoot some pretentious-looking arty visuals. Dripping paint onto the animation table, he created some odd configurations by using Q-Tips and paper clips. An amateur animator, he managed to create some rather interesting footage. I then edited the film from thirty minutes to just three and one-half minutes. Later, in a recording studio, Brooks improvised, using the voice of an elderly Jewish man. Finally, I edited the film, which took nearly one year to complete. Adding music at the final mix, I used a baroque composition by Johann Sebastian Bach.

The Critic was not the first of my films to satirize an art form that had been close to my heart. Such was also the case with *The Interview*, which had explored the subject of jazz. That animated film, from a recording by Henry Jacobs and Woodrow Leafer, depicts an interview with an inarticulate musician at a San Francisco jazz club. Having been a jazz trumpeter myself, I enjoyed poking fun at what I had considered to be a reflection of myself.

I later realized that the subjects of my short films have been closely related to my personal life and the opportunity to explore those themes motivated me.

The most personal element of my work, I believe, is expressed in the form of a "poor soul," which is a re-occurring character in my animated films, *Flebus, The Violinist* and *The Old Man and the Flower*. This lonely, grubby character is always struggling to communicate and find love, a reflection of myself. *The Violinist*, too, was inspired by my own struggles as an artist. I had been in psychoanalysis and was concerned whether analysis would affect my art or alter my spontaneity. The character of the violinist remains happy and grubby, so I concluded that analysis doesn't necessarily alter one's basic personality.

Animation historian Donald Crafton and others have said that animated films tend to be self-reflective and that animators often depict themselves in their work or create story ideas out of personal experiences. Crafton's thesis regarding my animated shorts appears to be true.

My first live-action short, *The Shoes*, continues with the theme of my animated films. Again, I deal with the poor soul character. The starring role in *The Shoes* was originally to have been played by Jackie Gleason, but was eventually given to Buddy Hackett. The live-action character played by Hackett was much like my animated characters. He was chubby, lonely, sad and funny.

Despite its similarities to earlier works, *The Shoes* marked a turning point in my career. I was becoming more interested in adult subjects and reaching broader audiences as well as dealing with a greater variety of themes. Inasmuch as I found animation to consist mostly of humor, I became more interested in drama and serious concepts.

My experience with *The Shoes* and my newly earned Oscar for *The Critic* were key factors in Columbia Picture's decision to encourage me to direct live-action films, the first of which was *Harvey Middleman, Fireman* in 1965. I wrote, directed composed the score and produced that feature, starring Gene Troobnick, Hermione Gingold and Charles Durning. After that movie, I left animation behind me and became involved with other aspects of the entertainment industry by developing several live-action projects, including the movie, *Bullitt*, starring Steve McQueen, which I partnered with producer Phil D'Antoni. I subsequently directed and produced a "magazine" film compilation called *Dynamite Chicken*, featuring Richard Pryor, Paul Krasner and Peter Max.

After directing and producing a super 16mm feature entitled *Blade*, starring John Marley, Karen Machon and Morgan Freeman, I used that film as a sample to break into the television industry in Hollywood where I directed television pilots and several TV shows. My special interest in the detective genre, which had developed with *Bullitt*, led to my directing numerous television segments, such as "Hawaii Five-O," "Kojak," "Policewoman," even "Dallas."

ARTICLES BY ANIMATION PROFESSIONALS

JOHN LASSETER, *Computer Animator and Director*

NICK PARK, *Animator Director*

BILL MORITZ, *Animation Teacher and Writer*

BILL HANNA, *Animation Director and Producer*

PABLO FERRO, *Director, Editor, Animator and Producer*

JULES ENGEL, *Painter, Animation Artist, Filmmaker and Teacher*

BILL MELENDEZ, *Animation Director and Producer*

BETISLAV POJAR, *Animation Director and Filmmaker*

HERBERT KLYNN, *Artist and Animation Producer*

FRED PATTEN, *Writer and Animation Reviewer*

BRUNO BOZZETTO, *Animation Director and Producer*

EMRU TOWNSEND, *Animation Filmmaker, Writer*

STAN LEE, *Cartoonist, Animation Writer and Producer*

AL BRODAX, *Animation Writer and Producer*

DEBRA KAUFMAN, *Animation Journalist*

NOEL BLANC, *Animation Director and Producer*

LINDA SIMENSKY, *Corporate Animation Executive*

JOHN CALLAHAN, *Writer and Cartoonist*

IRWIN BAZELON, *Composer, Conductor and Writer*

JAN LENICA, *Artist, Teacher, Animation Director and Producer*

JOHN LASSETER
Computer Animator and Director

In 1937, Bill Tytla, who animated and directed the beautiful "A Night On Bald Mountain" sequence in *Fantasia* said, "There is no particular mystery to animation. It is quite simple and like anything that is uncomplicated, it is about the hardest thing in the world to do!"

I have always had a passionate interest in animation, especially computer animation. While at the California Institute of Arts in the late 1970s, I produced two animated films, *Lady and the Lamp* and *Nitemare*, each winners of the Student Academy Award for Animation. In the mid-nineties, while vice-president of Creative Development at Pixar, an independent production company, I got to direct my first animated feature, *Toy Story*, the first such film to be produced entirely with computers. *Toy Story* went on to receive a Special Achievement Oscar.

Toy Story

Computer animation is an artistic medium which has grown out of science. But most of the images and animation created in this new medium were produced by the scientists who wrote the software tools, which is something like having all the paintings in the world created by the chemists who made the paint.

The most important thing to understand, in my opinion, is that computer animation is not an art form unto itself. Animation is the art form. The computer is merely another medium within this art form, as are pencils, clay, sand and puppets. In fact, I think of the computer as a big, expensive pencil which uses electricity. Sometimes it takes several people to operate the pencil. But until it is grasped by the hand of an artist, it is as useless as a pencil. Computer animation is not accomplished by computers any more than clay animation is created by clay.

Animation is not only an art form, rather it is a method of communication and a means of entertainment, an art form wherein ideas must be visually communicated. To communicate ideas clearly by visual means, one must first learn the fundamentals of graphic design, which is the vocabulary and grammar of graphic communication.

You must design your image so that it communicates your idea clearly. But visually communicating an idea is not enough. It should also be interesting and entertaining. Once this is achieved, you can be sure that your idea will have far more impact and the audience will both absorb and retain it.

As soon as an image starts to move, the principles of animation take effect. In the computer animation industry, one might think that to animate means to move an object from point A to point B. But the dictionary definition of the verb animate is "to give life to." In order to give life to movement, one cannot just move an object without reason. Every movement in an animated scene must have a reason for being. That is the basis for character animation. One must learn animation's fundamental principles, such as timing, staging, anticipation, flow through, squash and stretch, overlapping action, slow in and slow out, etc.

So often in the computer animation field, people with little animation experience will sit in front of a computer merely moving a few objects around and in doing so, consider themselves to be animators. Whether drawn by hand or computer, the success of character animation lies in the personality of the characters. Without an underlying conviction, the actions of a character are merely a series of unrelated motions. But with a thought process to connect them, actions bring a character to life. Strong characters and a compelling story, rather than technological advances, are what make an animation project great. It was Chuck Jones, who said, "All great cartoon characters are based on the human behavior we recognize in ourselves."

With all four of my short films, I strived to integrate human characteristics into the objects I chose as my subjects. In *Luxo Jr.*, a little lamp steals the spotlight with his playful antics. *Red's Dream* reveals what a lonely unicycle dreams about. In *Knickknack*, a glass-domed snowman is undone by his machinations to join a lively crowd.

I believe that *Tin Toy* was the first computer animated film to win an Academy Award because Tinny, the wind-up toy, managed to humorously and poignantly convey so many human emotions. All of the objects in the film have their own personalities and raison d'être, which serve to propel those films and make them memorable.

The principles of filmmaking, or film grammar, are vital to movies as a whole. How the story is constructed, the staging and pacing of action as well as the editing, are just some of the principles involved. If an idea does not further the story, no matter how compelling it may be, it should not be there. Everything within a single frame of film, the characters, the object, the background, even the space around the objects should be there for a purpose.

Computer animation is unique in that it combines the techniques of graphic design, animation, story writing, live-action filmmaking and computer science. But as with any artistic medium, the most vital element is creativity.

NICK PARK
Animator and Director

Like many other animators, my fascination with animation started at an early age. I was born and grew up in Lancashire, England, where artistic ability was not exactly considered to be an asset: It might lead to an interesting hobby, but not to a 'proper job.'" Luckily, I was born into a family with more imagination than this. They themselves were creative, and my parents have encouraged my siblings and me for as long as I can remember. My mother remembers quite clearly how, at the age of two, I drew a beautiful train in permanent ink...all around her brand new kitchen unit!

At school, I lacked both interest and ability in academic subjects. Art was by far my strongest subject. This was recognized and supported by my parents and a few of my teachers. Come to think of it, the only other subject I enjoyed was English, especially writing essays and stories, either science fiction or comedy. But it was making people laugh that gave me the most pleasure. I always loved comics, mainly *The Beano*, and drew my own characters and strips. My school exercise books were usually covered with cartoons, much to the dismay of the teachers. Once, for art homework, I even tried handing in a full-colored cartoon, an endeavor in which I had invested much effort and pride. The teacher's response was: "Cartoons are for children. You must take your art more seriously!" Being a strong-willed kid, this dismissal of cartoons made me determined to prove that drawing cartoons was in fact a way of taking art seriously.

Then at breakfast one morning, I read on the back of a cereal packet about a competition to make a simple zoetrope. The prize was a Super-8 movie camera and projector, so I entered the competition, dreaming of the films I would make if I won. At the time, I was

41

inspired by films featuring dinosaurs, the film *King Kong*, and all the animation of Ray Harryhausen. I even had my own collection of dinosaur figures. I didn't win the competition, but the idea of making films was now firmly planted in my head.

I often wonder what would have happened to my career if it wasn't for the discovery, at the age of thirteen, of a single-frame/animation button on my mum's standard 8mm Bell & Howell cine-camera. All at once, a number of things seemed to fall into place: my obsession with drawing cartoons, my desire to make movies, cartoon animation on television, stop-frame puppet and monster movies, and now, my mum's camera. I was also inspired by a documentary showing how Walt Disney started off by drawing a little mouse character. All in all, I felt as though I were being drawn in a certain direction, one in which I was more than willing to go.

My father, a photographer, set me up with a tripod and showed me which end of the camera to look through. In my usual obsessive way, I avoided planning anything, and chose for my first film the most laborious method possible. Using a cheap notepad and starting at the back, so that I could trace each successive drawing, I very crudely brought to life Walter the Rat, a character I had drawn previously in strip form. In his screen debut, Walter sauntered along, drank from a bottle of cider, and keeled over. Beginning, middle and end--a story. Although it was crude, the Walter film took an entire week to produce. Unfortunately, the little film got lost at the lab and couldn't be traced. I did not realize it at the time, but this was just a taste of the frustrations of an animator. Undaunted, I decided to have another go at it, this time using a quicker method. It starred Walter and his bottle of cider again, but this time using felt cut-out characters on a felt-covered background (my mother being a seamstress meant that I had an endless supply of felt trims). The film, *Rat and the Beanstalk*, lasted only two minutes, and featured Walter climbing the beanstalk, finding a bottle of cider in the clouds, and being chased by a giant.

Gradually, my catalog of films increased. I would spend evenings and weekends making animated films in my makeshift attic studio. Few of these works reached completion, but I considered them experiments in various forms of animation. My major influences at that time I varied between using paper cut-outs, puppet and clay animation, and cel animation. As I couldn't afford cels, I used tracing paper and a homemade peg bar. My major influences at the time were Terry Gilliam's abrupt cut-out animation for "Monty Python," and Bob Godfrey's shakily-drawn "Rhubarb" series. I also tried puppet and clay animation. New characters emerged, but Walter did make another appearance. *Walter Goes Fishing* was my first puppet film, and included my first piece of clay animation, in the form of Walter's nameless pet worm--all filmed in direct sunlight in my dad's garden shed.

Once news of my efforts leaked out to my English teacher, Mr. Kelly, he immediately took an interest and insisted that I show my work to the entire school at the end of our term. To my utter amazement, the screening went down a storm, as they say. Around the same time, I entered a youth competition sponsored by the BBC, and although I didn't win, they wanted to show my film, *Archie's Concrete Nightmare*, on national television. This meant instant fame at school, and at the tender age of fifteen, I thought I had reached the pinnacle of my career. I took a summer job at a chicken-packing factory to raise the money to buy my own Super-8 camera, and continued industriously making movies at home while studying Foundation Art. Again, I did not mention my interest in animation to any of my tutors. That was probably because of my early experiences at school. I still didn't believe that animation could be taken seriously as a career, and especially as an "art." My tutors were incredulous that I'd had this passion and not mentioned it, and they and my parents encouraged me to apply for a degree in Animation.

In those days, West Surrey College of Art and Design offered the only degree course in animation. The school was located in the south of England, and I couldn't even afford the train fare for an interview! Instead, I opted for Communications Arts studies at Sheffield College of Art and Design. The course was loosely structured with a fine arts bias, and we had access to some basic 16mm animation equipment.

In addition to learning more about live-action filmmaking, I worked on three short pieces using chalk and blackboard, puppet, and clay animation. Two of these were not completed. But I nevertheless gained my BA degree in Fine Art and Communication Arts, and a place at the National Film and Television School in Beaconsfield, near London.

The first year involved training in live-action filmmaking, and I specialized in animation for the final two years. The new animation wing was in its infancy and sparsely equipped. It was there that I began work on *A Grand Day Out*, my first 35mm film using clay animation. The film starred Wallace and Gromit, two characters taken from my earlier sketchbooks in Sheffield.

After eighteen months, with the film still only half-finished, I realized that I had bitten off more than I could chew, and my student grant money ran out. Fortunately, at that point, I received a work offer from Peter Lord and David Sproxton in Bristol at Aardman Animations. They also offered to help me complete *A Grand Day Out*, in collaboration with the NFTS. I worked part time on *A Grand Day Out*, and part time on Aardman jobs, including commercials, short films, and pop videos, in addition to children's television such as "Pee-Wee's Playhouse." The result was that *A Grand Day Out* took another four years to complete. I eventually graduated with the completed film in 1989, after six years in production and having done most of the animation myself.

By the time *A Grand Day Out* was completed, Aardman had produced a series for Channel 4, based on sound tracks of ordinary people recorded speaking candidly. My contribution to the program was *Creature Comforts*, a series of interviews with inmates of an English zoo. This sparked off a batch of electricity commercials in the UK that gave the technique a very wide exposure, to the extent that the TV spots were better known than the film. Both *A Grand Day Out* and *Creature Comforts* were nominated for the British Academy Awards and a year later for the Oscars. *A Grand Day Out* won at the former, and *Creature Comforts* picked up the gold statuette at the latter.

Creature Comforts

It was strange for me, having worked on *A Grand Day Out* for six years, to see *Creature Comforts* completed within five months. It seems as though *A Grand Day Out* was just pipped at the post, not that it makes any difference. Although *A Grand Day Out* had a more low key success, it gathered strength from *Creature Comforts* and paid off quickly, as the BBC committed to making more "Wallace and Gromit" films.

What I really wanted to do next was to write another Wallace and Gromit adventure. With Bob Baker, I began working on *The Wrong Trousers*, a half-hour comedy thriller, my longest film yet. With a crew of twelve, it took us just over a year to shoot. The film went on to win a second Academy Award in 1994, as did 1996's *A Close Shave*, in which my heroes foiled dastardly villains by rescuing a herd of hapless sheep.

Wallace and Gromit

45

I consider myself a "filmmaker who animates," rather than "an animator who makes films," and I believe this comes from learning to survive largely on courses orientated toward live-action film crafts such as writing, directing and editing. I don't really draw a hard line between live-action and animation directing. For me, it's all storytelling on screen.

Overall, the most valuable aspect of training has been to make my own films without commercial pressure and to nurture my own style and ideas. It is the simple magic of making things come to life which gives me the same delight I had making my home movies, and which still inspires my work.

WILLIAM MORITZ
Animation Teacher and Writer

Since much animation involves filming graphic artwork, styles of painting and drawing naturally influence animated films, either by involving a painter in filming his own brushstrokes in order to give them life in time, or by adopting the look of various paintings for the graphic style of a cartoon, or by making painting itself the subject of an animated film.

The painter Walter Ruttmann extended his abstract canvases into the realm of time through animation in 1919. His first film, *Light-play Opus I*, premiered in theatres in April of 1921. Ruttmann had painted on glass, shooting a single frame of film after each brushstroke or changing the image by wiping something away. Since he had to use black and white film, Ruttman hand-tinted the prints to restore the color values of his painting. Oskar Fischinger, who was present at the premiere of Ruttmann's *Opus I*, devoted his whole career to abstract animation. Fischinger's color films from the thirties are often referred to as "living Kandinskys." His last film, *Motion Painting*, records in ten minutes the many years of thought and experimentation that went into the making of one oil painting. It won the Grand Prize at the Brussels Experimental Film Festival in 1949.

A parallel tradition in abstract filmmaking involves painting directly onto a film's surface. Len Lye and Norman McLaren began doing that in the mid-thirties in Britain. Harry Smith in the 1940s, Hy Hirsh in the 1950s and Stan Brakhage in the 1980s have continued exploring direct painting on film with great success.

In a representational mode, the great Polish animator Witold Giersz began animating oil painting on glass in 1960, creating a range of

47

impressive films from the vivid *Forest Fire* to the hilarious *The Red and the Black*. Caroline Leaf used painting on glass as the medium for her film *The Street* which depicts a child's perception of his grandmother's death in sophisticated images that simultaneously seem childlike as well as artfully stylized in the mode of Chagall or Picasso.

The conscious use of modern art dates back at least to the early 1930s. Berthold Bartosch adopted the expressionistic woodcut look of Belgian artist Frans Masereel for his 1932 film *The Idea*, which, in its exploration of poverty, strikes and political protest, was the first animation film dealing with a tragic theme. Bartosch's friends, Claire Parker and Alexander Alexeieff, invented a pin-screen to create the finely-shaded images for "A Night on Bald Mountain" in 1933, which suggests the pointillism of Seurat as well as Picasso's supple rendering of the human form. British painter Anthony Gross brought the elegant abstraction of Matisse and Bloomsbury artists Duncan Grant and Vanessa Bell to the witty *Joie de Vivre*, *Fox Hunt* and *Around The World In 80 Days*, which were all completed in the 1930s.

In the forties and fifties, UPA attempted to integrate the standards of modern art into the design and color of their cartoons, giving each film an individual character, including choosing movement suitable to a particular graphic style. This commitment to modern art culminated in a series of television cartoons aimed at teaching young people about the works of renowned artists.

Painting has also been the subject of numerous celebrated animated films of the last decade. Frederic Back's *Crac!* traces the history of French Canada over the last century by using a rocking chair as the protagonist and surrounding it with animated reproductions of famous Canadian paintings. Estonian animator Priit Parn's *Déjeuner Sur L'herbe* in 1987 chronicles the extremes through which four poverty-stricken people must go in a totalitarian bureaucracy to have a picnic in the park, culminating in their momentary transformation into the famous Manet painting. Dan McLaughlin's *God Is Dog*

Spelled Backwards flashes countless recognizable paintings in three minutes by shooting single frames of reproductions as depicted in Janson's *History Of Art*. Joan Gratz's stunning *Mona Lisa Descending A Staircase* reproduces numerous famous paintings, transforming one into another with single frames, shot as modifications in colored clay-- breathtaking proof of the degree to which so many masterpieces of art endure.

BILL HANNA
Animation Director and Producer

The year was 1930 and our country was going through the worst depression it had ever experienced. Unfortunately, I was experiencing that same depression. I had dropped out of college and was looking for the same thing millions of other Americans were looking for. . . a job.

Luckily, I knew a man working for a company named Pacific Title and Art in Hollywood. The company made titles and subtitles for movies and was financing a cartoon production company called Harman-Ising Cartoons which was owned and operated by Hugh Harman and Rudolph Ising. Now, I hope you can appreciate how the name Harman-Ising Productions formulated and I landed a job there. That was where I first met Friz Freleng and Walter Lantz. They were both renowned animators and I was hired as a "cel washer." A cel is the sheet of clear acetate which is placed over animation drawings, traced with India ink, then painted various colors on the reverse side. After the finished artwork was photographed, I would wash the ink and paint off the cels and they were used again and again until the scratches from the pens began to show up onscreen. It is interesting to find that many inked and painted animation cels are now being sold in art galleries for thousands of dollars.

Rudolph Ising was considered the night stalker and within weeks of being hired, I was spending most of my evenings working late with Ising on story ideas. Since I played the saxophone, I worked part-time with Hugh Harman whenever music was involved. By the end of my first year with Harman-Ising Cartoons, I had become head of the inking and painting department. Soon, I was working full-time with both Rudy and Hugh on stories and music and was able to create the timing and direction of the animation because of my musical experience. By 1936, I was writing and producing. In 1937, I was offered a job at MGM to produce and direct animation and couldn't pass up the opportunity. It was then that I met Joseph Barbera, an artist who MGM had hired out of New York.

Shortly, Joe and I started working together, combining our talents. My musical background had helped me to acquire a solid sense of timing and Joe was a prolific comedy writer. We were both sticklers for detail and together we produced our first *Tom And Jerry* cartoon. *Puss Gets The Boot* was nominated for an Academy Award and in 1943, we won an Oscar for *Yankee Doodle Mouse*. That turned out to be the first of seven such awards that *Tom And Jerry* cartoons would receive over the following nine years. Twenty years later, after more than 160 *Tom And Jerry* cartoons, MGM closed their animation department, so we opened our own studio and called it Hanna-Barbera Productions. It has since grown to be the largest animation studio in the world.

For the next thirty-five years, Hanna-Barbera Productions concentrated on producing cartoons for television. In addition, we made a few features for theatres which involved characters originally created for television, such as Yogi Bear, the Flintstones, and the Jetsons. To name all the characters and animated series that Hanna-Barbera created over the

years would take a lot of research, although I am sure that the number of cartoon series would approach one hundred and involve thousands of cartoon characters.

We are always looking for young animators with talent and vision, either fresh out of art or film school, or those who have been working in the

The Jetsons

field for several years. Today there are more outlets for the work we produce than ever before. Animation has come of age.

At the moment, both Joe and I are involved in the process of producing and directing animated cartoons, something we have been doing for the past sixty-five years. When I was a child and would misbehave, my mother used to say, "Enough is enough, Willy!" But I don't know if and when I will ever stop.

PABLO FERRO
Director, Editor, Animator and Producer

In 1947, I was a little kid milking cows and farming in the deepest part of the Cuban countryside. Twenty years later I was an American film-maker creating animation techniques for Madison Avenue in New York City.

After our family moved to Manhattan, I attended the School of Industrial Art, and with two friends put together a little animation studio in Brooklyn. Using a dog-eared library book by Preston Blair as a guide, we built our own animation boards and stand, enabling us to shoot artwork with a 16mm Bell and Howell camera that photographed single frames.

At the same time, I worked as an usher in a 42nd Street theatre that showed foreign films, and became friendly with the projectionist. It was there that I first saw UPA's *Gerald McBoing Boing*, which impressed me with its originality. I was even able to acquire a few discarded frames from that film, which my friends and I studied at great length.

Searching for a graphic style, I began creating EC Comic Horror Books and illustrating stories for Atlas Comics. When looking for an animation job, I showed my comics but was only able to get work in the inking department at one animation studio. Next, I landed a job in the animation department of a studio that produced black and white commercials. When that company changed hands, several Disney artists were brought in, among them Bill Tytla, who had directed and animated the "Night On Bald Mountain" sequence in *Fantasia*. From Tytla, I learned a great deal more about the art of animation.

While working at various studios in New York, I developed my own style, and together with two partners formed Ferro, Mogubgub and Schwartz. We produced commercials for major firms and won many national and international animation awards. I later founded Pablo Ferro Films. Fortunately, my early use of multiple screens on television, and the quick cut technique (graphics combined with live-action and animation), came to Stanley Kubrick's attention, and he hired me to do the titles, trailer, and opening sequence for *Dr. Strangelove*. That assignment led me to creating numerous titles, logos, trailers and special effects for such films as *Midnight Cowboy*, *Harold and Maude*, *A Clockwork Orange*, *Stop Making Sense*, and *The Thomas Crown Affair*, for which I developed the use of single projected multiple screens. I also made my acting debut playing an Indian with severe back problems in Robert Downey's *Greaser's Palace*.

In the mid-sixties, after Sony developed the first black and white reel to reel system, I utilized their equipment to produce a series of short films for a television documentary series. Among the pieces I created were; "The Bridge," "The Lawyer," "Five Minutes Late," and "The Inflatable Doll." In that instance, utilizing video play-back enabled me to get better performances from actors, and saved considerable production time.

Settling in California, I continued to design titles and sequences for feature films, including *Beetlejuice*, *Dark Man*, *Philadelphia*, *The Addams Family*, and *To Die For*. Eventually, I was able to finance and direct my first live-action feature called *Me, Myself and I*, whose screenplay by Julian Barry I had commissioned years earlier. Also, among my credits is the Rolling Stone's *Let's Spend The Night Together*, which I created in association with Hal Ashby.

Looking back at my varied career, I think of show business like a roller coaster ride, in which only perseverance keeps one hanging on, while knowing how to survive, so that you can continue creating.

JULES ENGEL
Painter, Animation Artist, Filmmaker and Teacher

Experimental filmmaker Len Lye said, "Animation art is concerned with movement through space and with time has become the most important element of the 20th century. It took till this century to finally discover the art of movement."

Jules Engel

Experimental animation is a personal vision. It becomes a concrete record of an artist's self-discovery.

My particular emphasis has been to concentrate on the development of a visually inspired dynamic language, independent of literary and theatrical traditions, demonstrating that graphic choreography is capable of non-verbal truth. I have not sought out narratives to bring about graphic expression. Instead, I have chosen to convey ideas and feelings through movements which cannot be transposed into voices and words. Letters forming languages of specific cultures are not my means of expression. My voices and words are lines, squares, spots, circles and varieties of color. Though sometimes difficult to comprehend, these are the keys to the pictures.

In that regard, French poet Guillaume Apollinaire evoked an art beyond static painting and cinematographic representation, an art "which attracts those who are skilled in responding to movement, to color, to flow, to convergence and contrast."

It was not animated films which attracted me to the art of movement. My fascination and inspiration came from watching the Ballet Russes de Monte Carlo, where I discovered the artistry of movement found in classical dance. Through the choreography of George Balanchine and the dancing of Tamara Toumanova, Danilova, Baronova, David Lichine and Leonide Massine, my own vision began to emerge. The spectacular unity of body, spacing, choreography as well as music, conveyed with perfect precision, displayed infinite possibilities of gesture.

Another avenue opened for me with the dance of Martha Graham. In her work, I perceived how a more contemporary art could lead the way to new visions in movement, where each audience member participates in creating meanings from an emotional flow.

With the concept of movement as a universal expression, I have drawn on sources from diverse visual disciplines for inspiration, painters such as Wassily Kandinsky and Piet Mondrian, sculptors like David Smith and Alexander Calder with his perpetual moving mobiles. Such contemporary artists have been stimulating resources and references.

Movement itself is the content. It should include pause and silence. Do not merely look at movement, feel it. My work is abstract, but it contains an organic element. Instead of explaining, it helps one discover answers through pure feeling.

Since 1969, I have animated and produced more than thirty abstract films in which I generally create the graphic choreography from my own sense of timing. Experimental animators such as Oscar Fischinger and Norman McLaren have been motivated by music. Their work can be thought of as "visual music." I call my films "art in motion."

Occasionally I have been asked to make "films to music," such as when the Walt Disney Studios asked me to storyboard the Chinese and Russian dances for their new film, *Fantasia*. After consideration, I decided on a simple approach. Envisioning the characters as abstract shapes, I gave them color and movement in a restricted space. My only challenge was to convince the Disney artists to accept a black background without texture. In my opinion, the rhythms and motions to music were enhanced by such a background which removes screen corners so that shapes appear to move as though floating in space.

The animation industry was reticent about using color in the same manner as contemporary painters. Being one of the founders at UPA, I helped that studio become a place where artists could be innovative with color and expand the medium creatively. Color can create space and it can be dramatic or expressive in any form of implication.

Experimental film offers a magnificent opportunity to investigate space and time photography as well as composing in space for the spatial disintegration of forms. Composing in space also encompasses the flow of rhythms and forms.

Successive, transformable and ephemeral forms are able to disappear from view then re-form. One may arrest motion, slow motion, fragment images and change the surface of the screen or the exterior rhythm, even employ cubist composition. The potential is unending.

I am not bound by theory. I am conscious of the shapes and forms I work with, how they grow and develop inside film space and time. I am aware of their action, which presents me with avenues to move forward, to control, to evolve and finalize. Such work is not realized through mathematical formulae. It is gained through visual trial and error. It is a process of perception, a process of discovery.

BILL MELENDEZ
Animation Director and Producer

Perhaps I was fortunate in that I started my career in animation and film production purely by accident. Like many children, I naturally took to drawing. Unlike many children, however, I never outgrew that compulsion. Long after my childhood friends had stopped drawing for fun, I continued drawing seriously, or so I thought.

Bill Melendez

When I attended high school, rather than opting for an art curriculum, I chose mathematics. I arrogantly assumed that I could already draw, so I didn't need to take classes in drawing! After high school, in the midst of the depression, I faced resistance from those unwilling to hire uneducated artists. Then I had heard that a studio headed by Walt Disney was looking for young artists to serve as apprentice animators. Although I figured the position was not challenging, I hurried over to apply.

At that time, the Disney Studios were about to release its first animated feature film entitled *Snow White and the Seven Dwarfs*. Newly hired, I was shocked to discover that I was not up to the caliber of the many artists who surrounded me. Fortunately, the studio offered ongoing nightly art classes. There were life drawing classes, action analysis classes and animal drawing classes. It was simply the best thing that had happened to me. The teachers were incredibly stimulating both philosophically and artistically and they encouraged us to study art history as well. I bought art books, everything from the Renaissance to the Romans, Greeks, Etruscans and Egyptians. And the more I

61

studied, the more fascinating the prospect of animating life became. I became fascinated by all aspects of the medium and discovered that by marrying visuals to music and sound, my two-dimensional drawings could be magically transformed into three-dimensional sights and sounds.

The animator acts out a scene as he choreographs it. That opened up two areas of intensive study for me, music and dance. We were now working on *Pinocchio* and that experience was also invaluable. I learned as much from the work of those around me as I had from our class instructors.

The Walt Disney Studios trained us to animate as closely as possible to real life. Years later, at UPA, my colleagues and I attempted the opposite approach. We would caricature life like cartoonists rather than imitate it as does a camera. We tried to reject anthropomorphic subjects and decided to animate human characters in a stylized fashion. Those were exciting times, and artists such as John Hubley and Phil Eastman came up with a philosophy which grew from the realization that animation is an expressive and not purely a mechanical medium.

Like all artists, those involved in animation as actors through drawings, or as directors through film, must be engrossed in life around us, in all its aspects. Without that involvement, we risk losing control of the things which make creativity possible and our best work seems to emanate from individuals concerned with and involved in their society, whether through theatre, music, art, or politics.

Today, over fifty years after I first applied as an animator at the Walt Disney Studios, I look back in wonder at how much I have enjoyed my life's work.

Animation is the illustration of an action within a story. Working to bring that story to life is an exciting challenge.

I have directed and animated hundreds of commercials and won seven Emmy awards as well as directed five feature films. Of those, *Dick Deadeye*, *Snoopy Come Home* and *The Lion, The Witch and the Wardrobe*, are my personal favorites.

Peanuts

BRETISLAV POJAR
Animation Director and Filmmaker

In the first half of the century, when American film animation was achieving world success with productions from studios such as Walt Disney, Max Fleisher and Warner Bros., European animation barely existed. As a Czech, I lived in a country which did not produce animated films. I was part of that generation of Czech animators who started evolving their own techniques and styles after the Second World War. In that regard, I am a self-made man.

In 1942, after finishing high school, I tried to find a job because the Germans had closed the universities. So, I joined a newly-formed cartoon studio called AFIT, working as a designer. The owner was an Austrian architect with ambitions to become something between a European Disney and Richard Wagner. He liked to do operas in cartoon. Unfortunately, he had a very limited imagination. Everything we drew was rotoscoped from poorly-acting opera singers. The results were awful. At the same time, we were learning basic animation by secretly studying a few prints of Disney films. In any event, with the escalation of the war, the studio closed after one year.

Immediately after the war ended, the people from AFIT established the first Czech cartoon studio, Bratri v Triku. I worked there as an animator while attending art classes at the university. Within one year we had developed our own style of cartooning, different from mainstream American animation. Our films were based more on story than on comic characters, while our graphic style was taken from that of Czech book illustration. The main force behind this style was Jiri Trnka, an excellent designer, painter and set designer who was invited to be the artistic director. Although Trnka was not an animator in the strict sense, he gave new direction to our work, making animated puppet films.

Historically, puppetry is a folk tradition among Czech people. Trnka started by working in a puppet theatre as a schoolboy. Even as a successful artist, puppets were his greatest love. Through the technique of frame-by-frame shooting in animation, Trnka discovered a new way to bring life to his wooden heroes. Consequently, after one successful year making cartoons in 1946, Trnka decided to leave to start a new puppet studio and he invited me to join him.

Apart from Trnka's experiences in the theatre which were applicable to film, our group of animators and craftsmen knew very little about three-dimensional animation. We only had a few puppets, two old cameras dating from 1929 and some equipment discarded from live-action productions. Nobody could help us. We discovered and invented everything as we made those films. We were enthusiastic, managing with each successive film to turn our wooden puppets into living stars. I began making my own animated films, from writing to animating and directing. *A Drop Too Much*, my second short animated cartoon, won awards at Cannes and other festivals, affording me recognition and a measure of success.

Despite my excursions into documentary films and live-action films for children, I worked with Trnka in Prague throughout his most fruitful years, including his most ambitious project, Shakespeare's *A Midsummer Night's Dream*. In the following years, I produced and directed most of my films, although not always with puppets. But I recall my collaboration with Trnka because it has given me the courage to explore and experiment both with subject matter as well as technical possibilities.

I have made fables, modern fairy tales, lyrical works and comedies, including social and political satires which had been received poorly by authorities, who for a long time forced me to make only children's films. I utilized the technique of semi-relief puppets and created Czech-speaking animated puppets which were successful in my homeland, but unsuitable for international distribution. In a small country, it is wiser to produce films without words. To make a good foreign language version of an animated film is a privilege reserved only for big production houses.

I continue to experiment, combining cut-outs and puppets with live-action film. The charm of animation, for me, remains the possibility of creating many different worlds. Everything is in my hands and depends upon my choices and inventiveness. Those choices may be close to reality or rather abstract. In many films, I attempted to make visual the nonsensical world of the soul. In *Night Angel*, I showed a world perceived by a blind man. The same wealth of possibilities apply to sound.

Because of the variety of work and freedom of imagination, I have enjoyed making personal, non-traditional films and exploring puppet animation. Puppet animation is the stepchild of traditional animation, so it is necessary to spend extra time and care to perfect that art form in order to compensate for years of neglect. To be able to accomplish this has been my good fortune because not everyone is able to work in this independent way.

Computers, media attention and music videos are increasing public interest, thereby transforming the field of animation. Who knows how things will appear tomorrow? To work in animation, it is no longer necessary to carve a road through the forest of the unknown. With a solid history, technological advances and schools of animation, an entire highway now exists. Evolution does not stop. Today, there are infinite worlds for young animators to explore.

HERBERT KLYNN
Artist and Animation Producer

I am often asked why it animation is so different than other forms of film technique, and why it is often chosen for a particular formats, such as educational or industrial films.

These styles may range from the wholly imaginative to the simplest diagrammatic representation. For this reason, educational and industrial films can benefit from graphic techniques that are used to convey information which cannot be rendered representationally.

The ability of animation to creatively use color offers a great advantage. Color may be used to emphasize certain aspects of action to emphasize a point, or may be used symbolically to indicate a mood or feeling. Seldom used non-representationally in live-action filmmaking, color is frequently used in animation.

Versatility is another advantage of animation. One is completely free to reduce or accelerate the speed of a process to make a point. In the same regard, sectionalization may be used to help clarify an operation stage by stage. Animation can even superimpose upon a living image a moving diagram that analyzes the working principles of a complex object, such as a piece of factory machinery or techni- cal equipment. Together, with the utilization of sound effects or music, such techniques have the capacity to illustrate principles to promote learning.

The use of character animation may also be helpful in conveying infor- mation since it allows one to interject humor into an otherwise serious presentation of material and often helps to engage an audience.

Animation can adapt itself to virtually any subject, and has the potential to bring insight to a wide variety of material with its unique voice.

FRED PATTEN
Writer and Animation Reviewer

Having been a professional writer and reviewer of both American and foreign animation since the sixties, I was the co-founder of the first American fan club for Japanese animation in 1977. I now work with Streamline Pictures in Los Angeles, a company that acquires Japanese animation and dubs it into English for American theatrical and video distribution.

Japanese animation has recently emerged as a new cult category in American popular entertainment. It is especially popular with audiences who enjoy action-adventure science-fiction movies and super-hero comic books.

This unique art form was introduced into America in the late 1970s, when the Japanese community television channels in several major cities began showing giant robot super-hero cartoons with English subtitles. The first commercial VCRs also appeared at that time, allowing high-school and college fans to record them. During the next decade, the popularity of Japanese animation spread quickly.

The Japanese produce as much juvenile cartoon programming as the Americans do. But there is also a tremendous amount of adolescent and adult animation, including pornography. What has become known in America as Japanese animation is the science-fiction and adventure extravaganzas, whose effects would be exorbitant to produce in live-action.

After World War II, Japan was flooded with American movies, television and comic books. The first Japanese postwar animated films were feature-length dramatizations of the best-known Asian folk tales

71

adapted for children with lots of humor and cute animals. On the other hand, television animation emulated the American super-hero melodramas. Many of those Japanese cartoons were brought to America, such as "Astro Boy" and "Kimba, the White Lion." American and Japanese television animation began to diverge when American television animation came under greater restrictions against violence in children's programming which was perceived as encompassing all animation, while the Japanese public was demanding animated storytelling suitable for adults.

The most simplistic dramatic animation depicts a story that can be told as well in live-action as in cartoon form. A common cinematic gimmick in these films is an animated lens-flare in brightly-lit outdoor action scenes. More imaginative direction takes advantage of the potentials of animation even when the stories are mundane. The feature *Golgo 13* is a hard-boiled crime drama with no fantasy elements other than the protagonist's ability to survive innumerable death traps. But a nighttime automobile chase through downtown San Francisco becomes a surrealistic light-show of the reflections from neon signs wrapping themselves around the speeding cars. *Fist of the North Star* is a martial arts drama in which the fighters often move in slow-motion with colored streaks flashing from their fingertips, color-coded to indicate the moves of the different warriors, while the backgrounds fade into obscurity so that the focus remains on the battling antagonists.

The directorial reverse of this is the use of animation to present seemingly straightforward action into futuristic or fantastic settings which would be impossible to film in live-action without elaborate special effects. There are numerous inexpensive animated science-fiction adventures that resemble cheap sci-fi movies. But the "Mobile Suit Gundam" television and theatrical series remains popular because of the attention to detail and the realism of the space battle scenes and space-station environments, which reinforce the sophistication of the complex interplanetary geopolitical melodrama.

72

Japanese animation is beginning to have a greater influence in America in a variety of ways. Peter Chung, creator of the "Aeon Flux" cartoons on MTV's "Liquid Television," has been a fan of Japanese cartoons since his student animation days. A strong Japanese influence has been acknowledged as inspiration for the "dark deco" look of both live-action film and animated television versions of the Batman tale. Many of the leading Japanese cartoon directors, such as Hayao Miyazaki, Rin Taro, Katsuhiro Otomo and Yoshiaki Kawajiri, are studied by the new animators in the cartoon industry. And after Hayao Miyazaki's animated feature, *Ghost in the Shell*, earned highly favorable responses from industry professionals and critics, Walt Disney announced its acquisition of worldwide distribution rights to Miyazaki's most recent films.

More and more Americans are importing Japanese cartoon videos and laser discs to study animation techniques even when they cannot understand the language. It seems as though America is edging closer to the realization that "animation is not just for kids." A large market for creative action-adventure storytelling is on our animation horizon.

BRUNO BOZZETTO
Animation Director and Producer

My grandfather was a wonderful painter. He worked in an enormous and luminous room, covering the walls and ceiling with images. Whenever I visited him, I recall being struck by the pungent odor of turpentine, then by the gigantic paintings, but mostly of saints and madonnas which dwarfed me from the highest reaches of his studio space.

I'm not sure what significance those memories have for me, however, I believe that our lives can often be affected by such experiences. At any rate, when I was a boy in Italy, drawing remained just a hobby. In high school and college I studied everything except art. I confess that even while admiring Walt Disney, my passion was not for animation, but for live-action films. I never missed a chance to escape to the local cinemas. There, I discovered that character and story were what kept the audience glued to their seats and that the success of a film was not based upon the fame and talent of the actors, but upon numerous other things, such as character, plot, photography, rhythm, performance, music and sound effects.

When I was fifteen years old, I started shooting documentaries and short narrative films with a Bauer Super-8 camera, using my school friends as actors. From those experiences, I learned the importance of framing, lighting, camera movement and editing, a task which I have always enjoyed.

When I started experimenting with animation at the age of eighteen, I had already acquired an understanding of the cinematic medium and was convinced that artwork was not the most important thing. Rather, the most important elements were theme, story and the movements of the performances as well as the animated characters.

75

For me, the talent of the animator does not lie in the ability to draw well as it does in knowing how to give life to the movements of the characters by exploiting, with intelligence and humor, the smallest movements along with appreciating the value of such things as facial expression and dramatic pause. In short, the animator must be an actor, endowed with humor combined with a strong rhythmic and aesthetic sensibility.

Perhaps if I had watched only the Disney films, I would never have had the courage to make the leap of faith into that type of work. Disney films fascinated but intimidated me by their level of perfection. Such a degree of excellence seemed inaccessible to me.

Encouragement and stimulation for me came through a few short animated films by the National Film Board of Canada. Those were *Romance of Transportation* by Colin Low and *Blinkity Blank*, which was drawn directly on film by Norman McLaren. Ultimately, the coup de grâce came from The Walt Disney Studios in the form of an anamorhhic movie entitled *Toot, Whistle, Plunk And Boom*. That wonderful film was directed by Ward Kimball and it was *Toot, Whistle, Plunk And Boom* which convinced me that I could actually recount intelligent stories based on fantasy as well as daily life by using very simple drawings and animation techniques.

Shortly thereafter, with the financial help of my father, I acquired a movie camera and a Moviola. I then founded the animation studio from which many talents would emerge, people such as Guido Manuli, Giovanni Mulazzani, Giuseppe Lagana and Maurizio Nichetti. There were many others who also had their start in that studio.

At first, only advertising work guaranteed the financial survival of a studio. But I acknowledge the value of that work because it taught me fundamental things about creating original ideas and about amalgamating them. Above all, work taught me about the organization and techniques of production. By forcing me to work within the framework of strict time limits and deadlines, I learned about "precision." The creation of stories, themes and characters were especially stimulating and contributed to the creative growth of an entire studio.

Aside from commercials, I always based the characters in my animated work on the study of man, his obsessions and behavior along with the development of civilization as well as the natural world including the relationship with nature and animals. I believe that animated drawings are the most wonderful tools man has for dealing with such subjects. These tools offer an infinite number of views and angles from which to observe life's problems. We can study the world from afar or near. But we can reduce centuries to a few seconds and we can visualize dreams as well as thoughts. The effective use of this medium in original ways is a challenge for anybody. The animator is challenged to use creativity and humor while transforming his feelings into a story for an audience while sharing a view of the thousands of things which make up life.

If, as an animator, you succeed in providing an audience with a good time, you have accomplished a satisfactory job. But should you cause the audience to reflect upon what they have seen, you have accomplished even more. When I succeeded doing this, the pleasure I derived was enough to convince me that all the years I have dedicated to animation were well spent.

In addition to numerous short subjects, I have produced and directed three feature animated films at my studio in Milan. Those are *West And Soda, Vip, My Superman Brother* and *Allegro Non Troppo*. In 1987, I directed and co-produced a full-length live-action movie called *Under The Chinese Restaurant*.

EMRU TOWNSEND
Animation Filmmaker, Writer

Through the years, there has been considerable furor over what is acceptable or unacceptable in the visual media, especially regarding cartoons. The rise of political correctness and general paranoia as to the effects of cartoons on children have led to classic animation being pulled or expurgated on television, only to be replaced by cartoons that are painfully bland.

Being both black and a lifelong fan and student of things animated, I confess to sometimes feeling torn when it comes to the crude depiction of racial and ethnic groups in animation. In the past, Blacks, Asians, and Native Americans have received the short end of the caricature stick, or so it seemed to those of us at the other end of it. However, to censor every animated cartoon with a potentially offensive stereotype would be to eliminate some of the wittiest and most innovative works created. Some studios and networks have turned to editing out scenes from their libraries today recognized as offensive, but this is tantamount to revisionism. Still, there are some wonderful shorts out there that have never been viewed because of such considerations.

In viewing animation shorts from the early 1900s, one must remember that slavery had only recently been abolished in the United States. Still, a brand of humor that depends on making fun of another race or culture is difficult to watch today. One is even more ambivalent about allowing a little child to view such potentially painful material, especially if such is the only animated depiction of his or her group ever encountered.

Students interested in the history of questionable depictions of African-Americans might want to view Blackton's 1906 *Humorous Phases of Funny Faces*, McCay's 1911 *Little Nemo*, Harman and Ising's early 1930s *Sinkin' in the Bathtub*, Friz Freleng's 1938 short *Jungle Jitters*, Chuck Jones' *Inki and the Lion* of 1941, Bob Clampett's *Coal Black and de Sebben Dwarfs* from 1942, or Tex Avery's *Musical Maestro* from 1951. I imagine that each viewer will draw his or her own conclusions about the relative offensiveness of each of these works. At the very least, these films present an interesting historical context for exploring the subject of racial stereotyping in the United States.

Today, black stand-up comedians are prone to satirize white society from the classic position of an outsider, able to clearly see others' foibles. White audiences seem to appreciate this sharp humor as much as do black audiences. For what is caricature without exaggeration? I expect that as young blacks become more prominent in creating animation, they will bring with them this pointed satirical thrust as they view life both from within their culture and as they look out at the broader society. And this can only be a healthy thing. For what was missing most glaringly from early animation history was that sense of tit for tat, of each group's own voice clearly expressed in turn.

So where does this leave us? To broadcast or not to broadcast? I don't think that question can be answered here, but I do believe that we, the people, should discuss the subject rationally before it is decided for us. Knee-jerk reactions, whether to promote censorship or freedom of expression, will not work.

STAN LEE
Cartoonist, Animation Writer and Producer

I still recall my feeling of elation when as a child I would be in a movie theatre and the image of my favorite cartoon character materialized, full of exaggerated, improbable, silly and hilarious action.

After being exposed to my first full-length animated cartoon, *Snow White and the Seven Dwarfs*, I was hopelessly hooked. From that moment on, animation seemed like the greatest art form on earth.

Even during the years I spent as head writer, editor and art director at Marvel Comics, which was then known as Timely Comics, I never lost my love of animation. In fact, for a number of years, I supervised the production of dozens of animated-type comic books, such as *Terrytoons, Mighty Mouse, Super Rabbit, Buck Duck, Homer The Happy Ghost, Silly Seal* and *Ziggy Pig*.

Prior to that time, Marvel Comics, from its base in New York, licensed the rights to various Hollywood studios to produce cartoon versions for television shows adapted from our comic book characters, "Spider Man, "The Fantastic Four," "The Mighty Thor," "The Incredible Hulk," "Sub-Mariner" and "Iron Man."

While the majority of those cartoon shows were successful, I was never satisfied with the quality of story, characterization, or animation itself. Therefore, I decided it was time for me to become personally involved. Convincing the Marvel executives that we could do a better job of animating our own characters than anyone else, I moved to Los Angeles where I eagerly set about establishing my own animation studio.

81

Fortunately, we were able to hire some of the most talented animators, directors, storyboard artists and layout people in the business. Inasmuch as many kids were already Marvel fans, there was no need for orientation, so we were able to swing swiftly into production.

It was there, at our own animation studio, that I gained an appreciation of the tremendous amount of work, time and effort which goes into the production of animated cartoons. In the past, when making comic books, I was somewhat cavalier about editing both the dialogue and artwork. But no matter how many things required correcting, there was always time to make last-minute changes before we went to press. And I soon learned that television animation was different. In producing a network cartoon series, the pressure on each person involved with the show is incredibly intense.

Once the animation is completed, alterations can only be made at great expense and at the risk of ruining the production schedule. In animation, it is imperative that you be right the first time! Time and money are natural leveling factors and you can't re-do an animated scene as easily as you can re-draw a comic book page.

Yet think of how satisfying it is to work in a field where virtually any story you can conceive, no matter how wild or spectacular, can be illustrated, colored, put to music and brought to life with panache. The joys are immense.

Animation is the perfect blending of story and art, music and imagery, fantasy and myth. And today, with the advent of computer imaging, interactive technology and virtual reality, the field is limited only by the capacity of our imagination, which is unlimited.

AL BRODAX
Animation Writer and Producer

I have had the good fortune to work in animation as well as the
Broadway theatre, television and video. Promiscuous? Perhaps.
They are all connected in an almost incestuous way. But as in the case
of wives, lovers and children, in your heart of hearts there is always
one very special love. Mine is clearly animation.

As a child of the depression years, I found *Snow White and the Seven
Dwarfs* to be a refreshing break in the stormy clouds. Sitting in the
darkness of the theatre and breathing in the vague aroma of air condi-
tioning, I fell in love. In the 1950s, with the war and my university
years behind me, I eased my way into the mailroom of the William
Morris Agency. The agency was a veritable fantasyland, where I could
totally immerse myself in show business.

One of the company's clients was attempting to adapt some of
Sherwood Anderson's short stories into a play for Broadway. Luckily,
I knew Anderson's stories by heart, finding them brilliant in their
poetic simplicity. One day, while the client was seated in our recep-
tion area puzzling over his adaptation, I had the chutzpah to critique
Anderson's play. I had brought home the office copy to read over the
weekend, not having enough money to do much else. I had found lots
of shortcomings and didn't hold back. Our client appeared stunned
but interested. One week later, I received news that my analysis had
substance and I was asked to help write the final draft. Six weeks later,
I was one of three producers sitting in a Broadway rehearsal hall with
James Whitmore, Dorothy McGuire and Leon Ames. I was in heav-
en. I was also out of breath, running back and forth between
rehearsals and my job in the mailroom. I realized that plays closed
overnight and I still needed a steady income. But the play, entitled

Winesburg, Ohio, did not close overnight after all. It lasted for thirteen performances. On closing night, the play's publicist and I had an interesting discussion. He thought that I could have a promising future in show business but that I had a tendency to be drawn toward the poetic and esoteric. He suggested that I expand my vision by taking on something "dumb and popular," something like *Popeye*, for instance.

The 1950s were boomtimes for television. Promotions from mailroom to agent came fast and furious. By the mid-decade I was dubbed program developer. My mandate was to develop television programming for the agency's many stars. Along with two colleagues, I sat in a windowless office late into the night developing programs which indeed made it to prime time, such as the *Pulitzer Prize Playhouse*. Among the important clients on our agency's list was King Features Syndicate, a division of the Hearst Corporation, copyright owner of *Krazy Kat*, *Barney Google*, *Beetle Bailey* and *Popeye*. King Features, impressed by my enthusiasm, asked me to create a television and motion picture subdivision, that fortunately became successful. Ironically, my initial production involved the completion of over two-hundred "Popeye" episodes within eighteen months. Anyone with a modicum of experience in animation would deem that an impossible task. But thanks to the Hanna-Barbera technique of limited-animation and my naive approach, it somehow worked out. With strict controls over model sheets, writing teams and the utilization of domestic and foreign studios and most importantly, the voices of Jack Mercer and Mae Questel, Popeye and Olive Oyl, I completed the production within budget. The project was a success and brought joy to scores of kids as well as to the bookkeepers at the Hearst Corporation.

In the 1960s, we followed-up with "Krazy Kat," "Barney Google" and "Beetle Bailey." It was time to try new things and we did so with over thirty half-hour episodes of "The Beatles." The group's music was perfect for animation. A three-year run on the ABC network earned a fifty perfect share for its Saturday morning time slot, which was a rarity.

By the mid-decade, my grasp of animation was secure. The marriage of music, movement and story was something I wanted to expand upon. To create an animated musical became my goal. *Fantasia* had proven to be a masterpiece without a story and my desire to re-create that excitement with a solid story resulted in the production of *Yellow Submarine*. Fortunately, the music was available, but the script had yet to be written, so I summoned the best and brightest writing talents to complement the wonders of the Beatles' music. Seventeen treatments were written and dismissed by Brian Epstein, the Beatles' manager, although at least ten of them would have made marvelous movies. Ringo was insistent that the title of the movie had to be *Yellow Submarine*. In the end, together with Erich Segal, a Yale University professor, who later went on to write *Love Story* as well as other feature films, I plunged forward and wrote the screenplay which eventually became the movie.

The design by Heinz Edelmann was brilliant and not at all grounded in Walt Disney tradition. While Disney's characters were designed on a structure of circles, we thought that rectangles should become our foundation. As for backgrounds, we opted for a fine art approach, trying a form that would best present the mood of a scene, whether impressionistic, abstract, realistic or using painted photo negatives. It was the genius of the Beatles' music and the images rendered by a team of highly original artists that conjured up the magic of *Yellow Submarine*, considered by many an animation classic.

Ironically, that long-ago warning against indulging my tendency toward the poetic, indirectly led me to participate in one of the most creative full-length animation projects ever attempted, and for that I am grateful.

Animation, both traditional and computer-generated, along with a full measure of imagination, provides a rich canvas in the hands of gifted artists. Currently, a project called *Strawberry Fields* is on my agenda. There are already years of work behind that production, which is a live-action and a computer animation hybrid. We have a wonderful narrative, but I have the bureaucratic madness of studio machinations to deal with. But the magnificence of the dream is worth the quest.

DEBRA KAUFMAN
Animation Journalist

What is on the minds of computer animators today is creating completely realistic digital creatures, including human beings.

In the ten years that I have been covering the entertainment industry for the trade press, I have often written about computer animation as well as graphics and how such technology has been used in feature films. It seems hard to believe how far we've come in a relatively short period of time.

A survey of how computer animation and graphics developed in feature films shows the logic of an idea seemingly as farfetched as the digital actor. Prior to *Star Wars*, computerized effects were dismissed as being clumsy, unrealistic and inartistic. But *Star Wars* featured a digital motion control system that produced the film's astonishing visual effects. It was the first indication of what was to come. When the film was completed, George Lucas went to San Rafael, California and founded Industrial Light and Magic, quickly establishing a computer graphics division. But in the early 1980s, computers did not yet have enough processing power to create imagery fast enough to be realistic and economical.

In 1986, *The Adventures of Young Sherlock Holmes* was ILM's first attempt to bring a computer-generated image to life, just like the film's knight in a stained glass window who breaks out of a two-dimensional window into three-dimensional reality. At that moment, ILM's investment in computer graphics research and development came to fruition.

This same technique for generating computer images, then compositing them with live-action sequences on film that had been scanned into the computer, was further developed in *The Abyss*, which many experts think of as a visual breakthrough. Audiences could only marvel at the shimmering water tentacle that imitated human faces. Created as a computer wireframe model with photos mapped onto the geometry, the tentacle imitates water qualities by reflecting and refracting the environment around it.

In a similar manner, ILM created the striking, *morphing* chrome man in the widely seen *Terminator 2*. This film proved the power of computers to create dramatic and believable imagery, while seamlessly integrating such imagery with live-action footage. The computer-created chrome man was only one of the film's many computer-aided effects, which included the creation of totally new images using computer graphics imagery, the alteration of existing images through 2D image processing and the skilled combinations of both.

Jurassic Park was another leap forward. Until that film, the computer had been used to create objects and creatures that were obviously invented. Creating living, breathing creatures such as dinosaurs was a distinct challenge. Both biologists and computer animators will readily explain that all sentient beings are incredibly intricate, with a myriad of details, nearly impossible to replicate. It was also a challenge to create organic elements such as hair and skin in the computer. So an enormous effort and lots of computing power went into creating a realistic look.

Jumanji used digital techniques to create animals that roam the earth today, such as monkeys and a lion. That film pushed the benchmark up a significant notch, since, unlike with dinosaurs, we have first-hand experience about how animals such as monkeys or lions should look and behave.

That's exactly why creating a human being in the computer is a much more daunting proposition. It's not just about creating believable muscular structure or credible hair. Our brains are hardwired to recognize the many extreme subtleties of human motion and behavior. Even a minor detail that is "off" will ruin the end result.

Nonetheless, we've seen a few digital humans. *Jurassic Park* created a digital lawyer who was gobbled by a dinosaur. The pioneering facility known as Pacific Data Images, created a digital *Batman*, complete with flowing cape, who leapt off a building in *Batman Forever*. In both of those cases, the camera was far enough away and the shot was quick enough to make the illusion work.

As the digital actor becomes more possible, the debate begins in earnest about the technique's raison d'être. Some believe that the digital actor is best used to accomplish stunts too dangerous for a stunt person. They point out that a digital image which replicates the physical characteristics of a major star of yesteryear does not come with software to recreate that star's ineffable qualities of personality. In other words, even if we can create a believable Humphrey Bogart or Marilyn Monroe, the behavior of any computer-created Bogart or Monroe would be a mishmash of old movie clichés and the director's own personality. Not a very satisfying or believable combination.

One technique to animate a well-known actor is getting a lot of play. The ability to digitally composite existing footage with newly shot footage, as first seen in Diet Coke commercials featuring old footage of Humphrey Bogart and Gene Kelley with contemporary personalities like Paula Abdul, was used effectively in the film, *Forrest Gump* as well as "Trials and Tribble-ations," a thirtieth anniversary "Star Trek: "Deep Space Nine" episode. Although convincing, this technique often plays more like a trick than a legitimate exercise in believable drama because the director is limited by what the actor did and said in the old footage.

That does not mean that the animation community won't keep trying to create a digital "actor." It's a kind of Mt. Everest and as such, must be climbed. Motion capture systems have made it possible to capture a living actor's movements, which is then used to animate a 3-D model. Reportedly, certain well-known actors and personalities are creating motion-capture files of their movements as a kind of digital inheritance. Of course, as with cryogenics, time will tell whether or not the dead can be resurrected--and whether or not anyone will want to.

How far can we go? We'll all be witness to the attempts. The implications of the digital actor, its potential uses by politicians, corporations and the media, are too awesome, potentially even sinister, to imagine. Viewed in the context of an era in which the capability of all digital media is dramatically expanding into new and unconventional arenas, staying informed about what technology can do assumes a new, urgent importance. The fat lady hasn't sung yet, but when she does, she'll almost certainly have been created by a computer.

NOEL BLANC
Animation Director and Producer

Just imagine that you are in a darkened theatre. You are eight years old. It's Saturday morning. Up on the giant screen, to the cheers of your friends in the packed house, comes the Warner Bros. logo and its zany theme song introducing the greatest collection of cartoon characters the world has ever known.

© *Noel Blanc*

"Eh, what's up, doc?"
"Take it from me, Foghorn Leghorn, you're all washed up."
"Ooh, I taut I taw a puddy tat."
"How about we just talk about, about zee love, mes amis?"
"My life story, "A Duck is Born!"
"You'll be seeing stars if ya don't shut that beak. . ."
"A thee, a thee, a thee. . . a that's all folks!"

These are just some of the one thousand characters that my dad brought to life during his more than fifty year career, working on a variety of projects for numerous studios. By any measure, my father, Mel Blanc, is thought to be the greatest voice-over artist in film history.

After graduation from UCLA and a stint in the army, I returned to form a production company and creative think-tank with my dad. I have been in the animation and film business ever since. Together with my mom, Estelle, my dad had always encouraged me to study hard in school, however, growing up in the house that Bugs built,

91

meant being exposed to some of the great legends of the entertainment business, starting with Jack Benny, George Burns, Lucille Ball and Abbott and Costello, whom my dad worked with during the golden age of radio. Those talents in particular made a tremendous impression on me.

Watching and listening to my dad become each character was as fine an education as any animation director or producer could ever hope for. My father said that in order for a character to be accepted by an audience, he must be totally believable within the context of the production. This begins with creating exactly the right voice to match its scope and subtle shades. How should one go about creating exactly the right voice for a two-dimensional drawing? The vocal artist must communicate with the graphic artist who created the character, because it is the collective questions and answers which lead to establishing the subtext or story of the character. Like method acting, understanding the character's motivation when giving a voice to a drawing is essential.

Originally, Bugs Bunny was known as Happy Rabbit and had a rounded look with big buck teeth and a dopey voice. When Warner Bros. decided to change the character drawing of Happy, they asked my dad to create a new voice for him as well. After suggesting that the producers name the character after the animator who drew him, Bugs Hardaway, my father wanted to know what kind of a person Bugs Bunny would be and what would be the primary storyline for each Bugs Bunny cartoon. The directors said that Bugs would be a tough but lovable stinker who always won out no matter what. So my father decided on combining accents from the Bronx and Brooklyn. "Eh, what's up Doc?" was the popular phrase of the day. My dad felt it carried the right attitude for Bugs and suggested it as a signature line. He went on in this fashion until he had realized his character completely.

Creating animation characters depends on combining elements of design, story and voice into a seamless whole, regardless of format. In other words, what you may be doing in an ultra-modern, computer-based production lab really isn't different from what Bob McKinson, Friz Freleng and my father were doing in a cavernous building on the Warner Bros. lot, affectionately dubbed "termite terrace," some fifty years ago. Today, those same Looney Tunes characters whose voices my father created are heard by over two hundred million people around the world each day. Not bad for a smart-aleck rabbit, huh?

© *Warner Bros.*

LINDA SIMENSKY
Corporate Animation Executive

If you want to travel and see the world, working in the animation industry could be a good idea. My career in animation began in 1984 as an intern at the Nickelodeon programming department, and one of my first tasks was working on the dubbing of *Belle And Sebastian*, a Japanese cartoon about a boy and his dog in the French-Spanish Pyrennes. I recall chuckling about how international the show had become by the time we ran it on American television. At that point, most of Nickelodeon's animation programming had been acquired from other countries, which was unusual for American TV. Although many of us had grown up watching Japanese cartoons such as "Speed Racer," Americans generally assumed that all entertaining television was produced in Hollywood.

While completing my graduate studies at New York University, I moved from the programming department at Nickelodeon to the newly-created animation department, where my job included developing and assisting the production of animated pilot episodes and series. I soon discovered that working on American cartoons required a full knowledge of the international animation scene.

There are many levels of international involvement for each program produced, starting with the script and storyboard. At Nickelodeon, we went into each production with the knowledge that the program sales department would most likely sell the show internationally and that the show would be dubbed into many languages. When we worked on a specific episode, we kept this in mind, making sure there were no written words or signage in the backgrounds crucial to the plot or no slang in the dialogue, since it is sometimes impossible to translate.

There was a Program Enterprises Department, that focused on international co-productions and involvement. Because animation is so costly, often it is beneficial to find an international co-producer willing to finance a portion of the program. Nickelodeon worked with Ellipse, the production arm of a French television channel as well as a company called Canal+ to co-produce the animated series "Doug."

Television animation production usually involves an international component. Most animation that is produced for television in the United States is inked, painted and filmed in Asia. There are a number of studios in Korea, as well as in Taiwan, Hong Kong, China, Thailand and the Philippines that are set up to do this work for less cost than we could produce it in America or Europe. For the production of four programs, Nickelodeon and its associated production companies employed four different Korean studios.

In dealing with Korean studios, Americans must learn to communicate clearly and directly regarding animation with artists who may not understand a show's culture-based sense of humor, certain elements of plot or even the basic content, such as a story revolving around the game of football. A program's production bible reminds art directors and storyboard artists to keep in mind that their storyboard and direction notes should be written clearly and succinctly because they will be translated into the Korean language. This lends to additional challenges. But the overseas directors work closely with the Korean animators to make sure they understand both our stories and directives. Ironically, this gulf often indicates when the slapstick and movement are really working. If the Korean animators chuckle or laugh from looking at the action without reading the story or dialogue, we know that the gag is a good one. In fact, one reason animation has been internationally successful is that it can transcend so many boundaries, both cultural and linguistic. So much animation is based on action, movement and physical humor that it can work in many different cultures. Also, it can be easily dubbed when necessary.

Currently, I am Vice President of Original Animation at the Cartoon Network. There are three other Cartoon Networks, in Europe, Asia and Latin America and I work with the directors of programming, dealing with production questions, problems, acquisitions and search for talented animation creators from all over the world. Despite the similarities of programming, the channels have widely varying issues to deal with, ranging from competition to audience composition.

In the course of my career in animation development, production and programming, I always make time to visit local studios whenever traveling. Some of my more interesting excursions have involved visits to animation studios in Shanghai and Dublin. I feel that it is very important to understand the production capabilities and talents which exist in foreign countries.

Animation has always been part of the global village and progressive television networks have played a key role in bringing more international animation to TV screens in the United States than ever before. No doubt, there will be more international involvement as more cable channels are created.

If you are about to start a career in animation, it seems inevitable that no matter which area you specialize in, at some point your focus will be international.

JOHN CALLAHAN
Writer and Cartoonist

I grew up in a peaceful Oregon town and had a strict Catholic education. As a kid, I liked drawing and took special delight in teasing and ridiculing the nuns with my caricatures, but when I started drinking in my teens, my interest in cartooning waned.

Then, one night in 1973, shortly after my twenty-first birthday, I was out on a spree with a pal when our car hit an exit sign at ninety miles an hour. My spinal cord was severed and I have been paralyzed from the neck down ever since. I find the hardest thing about being a quadriplegic is the dependency one has on other people.

Cartoon by John Callahan

After leaving the hospital, I lived in nursing homes, then moved into an apartment. It was tough going, but eventually, I felt like drawing again and started cartooning, with my left hand guiding.

From the beginning, I have dealt with all sorts of touchy subjects including religion, anorexia, alcoholism, paralysis--you name it. The only criteria for me has been that my cartoons be funny. It took a while, but eventually some newspapers and magazines began to run my work and I have since had six collections published. I still get flack about my choice of material, but I believe there is a double standard for humor in America and I try to skewer that.

99

Pity and patronizing attitudes are abhorrent to me and to others I know in my situation. I find humor in all aspects of life. People who are suffering from a disease often create their own private jokes as a way of coping with pain.

Why not share the joke? The question of what is off-limits should not be defined by some over-protective special interest group. The audience should decide for themselves.

I've adapted some of my cartoons into animated short films. They've been pretty well received. And Robin Williams has optioned the film rights to my autobiography, *Don't Worry, He Won't Get Far On Foot*.

IRWIN BAZELON
Composer, Conductor and Writer

Having graduated from the School of Music at DePaul University, I went on to study composition with Darius Milhaud at Mills College in California.

Later, I arrived in New York City to begin my musical career and recall writing over three hundred letters to schools all over America, inquiring about obtaining a teaching position in music. Being unsuccessful, I subsequently took a job as a reservation clerk with the Atlantic Coastline Railroad and worked there for seven years while writing music every night.

Finally, I decided to quit that job and through a series of fortuitous introductions, managed to meet the chief executive at UPA in New York, who was looking for off-beat music for a series of animated spots the company was producing to promote the Alfred Hitchcock television show. As the execs listened to my music, I frantically used my voice to illustrate and imitate musical instruments and the studio hired me to compose a score.

I recall how I presented my compositions by utilizing a piccolo, xylophone, trumpet and tuba. That was a radical departure from the "jingle mentality" of numerous sound tracks written for commercials during that period. Nevertheless, my work was accepted, despite the objections of the account executive who didn't seem to appreciate the "different" sound of my music.

UPA coordinated my score with the animation and instead of usual orchestrations, I began to write compositions with unique musical combinations.

101

Soon, I found my work in demand on a scale I had never dreamed possible and was collaborating with highly creative art directors who were eager to employ contemporary solutions featuring diverse music. That led me to embrace documentary movies, art films, industrial movies, commercials, music for theatre and television programs, Probably most recognizable, was my eight second theme for NBC TV News, which ran on all public service programs in the sixties.

Fortunately, I found myself working with people who were aware of the difference between a composer and a non-composer, a score and a non-score. I began to write music quickly, efficiently and with assurance, without having to use the piano for trial and error compositions, but to hear it played immediately by the best musicians in the world, including members of the New York Philharmonic. In short, I had become a professional composer with confidence and a sense of pride.

I have since had the opportunity of conducting my music for both documentaries and animated movies as well as in concert halls.

My beginnings as a composer literally commenced with the compositions I wrote for animated commercials and short subject films. This gave me the opportunity to actually hear my music and to grow creatively.

JAN LENICA
Artist, Teacher, Animation Director and Producer

I have always liked moving on the outskirts of animation, penetrating regions situated far from the main routes. I find that it is challenging and amusing to ignore the rules, to blend together elements from opposing and unconnected fields, to blur boundaries. Throughout my career, I have been attracted to many commonplace forms held in disregard by those who work in more refined areas.

These remarks may seem innocuous today with the general integration of the visual arts. But I recall the time when painters and art critics scorned graphic art. In the 1950s I was fond of using non-graphic techniques in my artwork which was not compatible with the current printing techniques and I was criticized for introducing subjects into my posters that originated from painting, such as portraits.

Today there are few techniques that have not been influenced by poster art, eliminating the isolation of graphic design. Posters have returned to their source as they integrate multiple pictures on one subject.

The situation in films is somewhat different in that I have chosen a difficult position for myself. The ruling principals of supply and demand are ruthless in that everything that does not find its commercial place in the market. In the past, I thought that animated films could become an instrument of fantastic possibilities when dealt with by an artist. Film appeared to me as the most contemporary raw material, an unparalleled means of expression and a fruitful area of activity. I was not fully aware then of the enormous difficulties experienced by those who do not want to bow to the commercial system of filmmaking.

Cinema as an object and manifestation of art in time and movement has not yet found its sponsor or collector. But I envision a golden opportunity for film with the development of new techniques of reproduction in video cassette and laser disk. This may result in the level of distribution of all sorts of films that up to now only works of literature and music have enjoyed.

Having been born in Poland, I studied music and architecture in Warsaw during the late 1930s. I've worked in Paris and Germany, lectured at Harvard University, making both short and full-length works, experimenting with a variety of techniques throughout. I have been called an existentialist and compared to Kafka and Ionesco. In any event, I am now retired, though still a poster designer and animation filmmaker.

RECOMMENDED ANIMATION BOOKS AND FILMS

The following is a list of recommended animation books and films:

RECOMMENDED ANIMATION BOOKS:

Animation From Script To Screen, by Shamus Culhane, published by St. Martin's Press

Animation In The Cinema, by Ralph Stephenson published by Tantivy Press

Animation Journal, by Maureen Furniss, published by AJ Press

Cartoons, by Giannalberto Bendazzi, published by Indiana University Press

Cyberarts, by Linda Jacobson, published by Miller-Freeman

Design In Motion, by John Halas and Roger Manvell, published by Hastings House

Masters Of Animation, by John Halas, published by Home Vision

Of Mice And Magic, by Leonard Maltin, published by Plume Books

Talking Animals, by Shamus Culhane, published by St. Martin's Press

That's Not All, Folks! by Mel Blanc,
published by Warner Books

The Complete Guide To Standard Script Forms, by Cole and Haag,
published by CMC Publishing

Masters Of Animation, by John Halas
published by Home Vision

The Complete Film Dictionary, by Ira Koningsberg,
published by the Penguin Group

The Timetables Of History, by Bernard Gunn
published by Touchstone Publishing

The Animated Film, by Ralph Stephenson
published by Tantivy Press

The Complete Guide To Standard Script Forms, by Cole and Haag,
published by CMC Publishing

RECOMMENDED FILMS:

A Close Shave, from Nick Park, Aardman Animations.

A Midsummer Night's Dream, from Jiri Trnka.

Adam II, from Jan Lenica.

Aladdin, from Walt Disney Pictures.

Alice In Wonderland, from Walt Disney Pictures.

Barnyard Olympics, from Walt Disney Pictures.

Betty Boop Limited, from Max Fleischer Studios.

Chuck Amuck, from Warner Bros.

Cinderella, from Walt Disney Pictures.

Clay, The Origin of Species, from Elliot Noyes.

Crac! from Frederic Back.

Daffy Duck and Egghead, from Warner Bros.

Destination Meatball, from Walter Lantz.

Donald's Lucky Day, from Walt Disney Pictures.

Farmer Al Falfa's Twentieth Anniversary, from Terrytoons.

Flebus, from Terrytoons.

Going! Going! Gosh, from Warner Bros.

Is the Earth Round?, from Pritt Parn.

Just Mickey, from Walt Disney Pictures.

Kama Sutra Rides Again, from Bob Godfrey.

Lady and the Tramp, from Walt Disney Pictures.

Landscapes, from Jordan Belson.

Magoo's Puddle Jumper, from UPA.

Mighty Mouse and the Pirates, from Terrytoons.

Mighty Mouse and the Wolf, from Terrytoons.

Monsieur Tete, from Jan Lenica.

Night Angel, from Bretislav Pojar.

Night, from Walt Disney Pictures.

Oliver And Company, from Walt Disney Pictures.

One Hundred and one Dalmatians, from Walt Disney Pictures.

Peter Pan, from Walt Disney Pictures.

Pianissimo, from Carmen D'Avino.

Pluto's Dream House, from Walt Disney Pictures.

Pocahontas, from Walt Disney Pictures.

Popeye and the Pirates, from Paramount Pictures.

Porky's Romance, from Warner Bros.

Rain Drain, from Terrytoons.

Sleeping Beauty, from Walt Disney Pictures.

Snoot and Muttly, from Susan Van Baerle.

Speedy Gonzales, from Warner Bros.

Steamboat Willie, from Walt Disney Pictures.

Streams of Consciousness, from George Griffin and David Ehrlich.

The Adventures of Prince Achmed, from Lotte Reiniger.

The Apple, from George Dunning.

The Black Cauldron, from Walt Disney Pictures.

The Box, from Murakami-Wolf.

The Cactus Kid, from Walt Disney Pictures.

The Christmas Carol, from Richard Williams

The Critic, from Columbia Pictures.

The Dot and the Line, from MGM.

The Fox and the Hound, from Walt Disney Pictures.

The Hand, from Jiri Trnka.

The Idea, from Berthold Bartosch.

The Interview, from Columbia Pictures.

The Old Man and the Flower, from Columbia Pictures.

The Owl and the Pussy Cat, from Terrytoons.

The Red and the Black, from Witold Giersz.

The Street, from Caroline Leaf.

The Sword and the Stone, from Walt Disney Pictures.

The Three Little Bops, from Friz Freleng.

The Ugly Duckling, from Walt Disney Pictures.

The Violinist, from Columbia Pictures.

Tup Tup, from Zagreb Films.

We're in the Money, from Warner Bros.

When the Wind Blows, from Jimmy Teru Murakami.

When Magoo Flew, from UPA.

Who Framed Roger Rabbit?, from Touchstone Pictures.

Zana and Miri, from Vlash Droboniku.

BIBLIOGRAPHY

Beaver, Frank, *Dictionary Of Film Terms*, McGraw-Hill
New York: 1983

Barbour, Alan, *The Thrill Of It All*, The McMillan Company
New York: 1971

Benayoun, Robert, *The Films Of Woody Allen*, Crown Books
Paris: 1987

Laybourne, Kit, *The Animation Book*, Crown Books
New York: 1980

Halas and Manvell, *Design In Motion*, Hastings House
London: 1962

Jacobson, Linda, editor, *Cyberarts*, Miller-Freeman
San Francisco: 1995

Maltin, Leonard, *Of Mice And Magic*, Viking USA
New York: 1980

Williams, Vera S., *WASPS*, Motor Books International
New York: 1950

Wiley, Mason and Bona Damien, *Inside Oscar*, Ballantine Books
New York: 1986

GLOSSARY

A and B ROLL EDITING

A and B roll printing contains alternating segments of the original film which overlap each other when dissolves are required. The A and B technique enables dissolves and fades to be effected without going through another processing generation.

A and B ROLL PRINTING

A and B roll printing is accomplished with two or more rolls of film conformed and matching, with alternate scenes intercut with black leader. This process allows for checkerboard cutting, which eliminates visual film splices on the screen. It also permits single or double exposures, multiple exposure and hands-on re-editing by the frame.

AMBIENT SOUND

The natural environmental noise, or ambient sound, that surrounds a scene. Usually, environmental noises have their own sound track for mixing.

ANIMATION CAMERA

Used for filming animation, this camera is usually mounted on a stand with its optical axis vertical so that it looks down on the objects being photographed. The camera-drive meter allows the film to move forward one frame at a time.

ANIMATION STAND or CRANE

A precise, customized camera mount for animation usage, this stand or crane is capable of accurate gradations of movement above the art work, peg board or platen. This unit usually has capabilities for both subtle and complex moves.

ANIMATION TABLE

A flat table with a circular rotary inset, this transparent surface permits the cel, which is registered on pegs, to be turned to any angle for observations, matching, inking or painting.

ARMATURE

In animation and puppetry, an armature is the skeleton or framework upon which is placed the outer coating for a piece of sculpture. With sophisticated models made for special-effects photography, armatures are articulated and allow for various kinds of motion. Movement of the models may be created manually or by stop-motion.

AUTODESK ANIMATION PRO

Autodesk Animation Pro is a two-dimensional animation software program that is published by Autodesk Incorporated.

AUTODESK 3-D STUDIO RELEASE 2

A three-dimensional animation software program, Autodesk 3-D Studio Release 2 is produced by Autodesk Incorporated.

CD-ROM, CDTV, or CD-1 COMPUTER-AIDED WORKSTATIONS

The use of computers to create the geometric detail and labeling involved in product and architectural design and drafting. CD-ROM and CD-1 Computer-Aided Workstations consist of one or more work places that include a keyboard, a high-resolution display screen and either a light pen, a mouse, or a graphics tablet. Software in the workstation helps users create and manipulate drawings in either two or three dimensions and may contain details of characteristics and dimensions of parts as well as components that can be incorporated into drawings.

COMMODORE

Developed by the Phillips Corporation, Commodore was the first local storage disc which utilized CD-ROM standards.

COMPUTER-GENERATED ANIMATION

Computer-generated animation encompasses any animation created via computer. It is usually created with varied and highly sophisticated software for a hardware platform with immense memory capacity and speed.

CUE SHEET

A cue sheet is a log with columns that indicate to the re-recording engineer, during dubbing, where certain animation music, sounds and dialogue come in and how they are treated when combining them onto a single track.

DOLBY SOUND

Dolby Sound is a sound recording system developed in the during the 1970s, that, by reducing background noise, allows better fidelity for magnetic tape and optical sound tracks on film. The system accomplishes this by compressing the sound range during recording and decoding the signal by expanding, during playback, a level grater than the level of the noise. The stereo system itself operates on 35mm film through two optical channels which actually create four distinct sound tracks.

EXPOSURE SHEET, or BAR SHEET

An exposure sheet, or bar sheet in animation is a guide for the animator and cameraman, prepared by the editor and animator which indicates the position for each cel and the number of frames in which the cel should be photographed. The sheet also indicates the movement of the camera, transitions, as well as the position of the camera.

FLATBED EDITING

Flatbed editing refers to a table equipped for editing and is now frequently used instead of the upright Moviola. Despite their expense, they are often preferable to the Moviola, inasmuch as they treat film more gently, allowing it to be handled with greater speed and ease, creating more accuracy. Some tables can be used for both 16 and 35mm film. Editing tables are now manufactured allowing the transfer and mixing of sound, the editing of film and videotape as well as transfer onto a small translucent screen. Flatbed devices also permit the use of anamorphic lenses.

FRACTAL

Fractal art generation is a computer process that creates complex, repetitive, mathematically defined geometric shapes and patterns that are found in nature.

GAUGE

The gauge refers to film that is measured in millimeters. The standard animated film measurements are 8, **16, 35** and **70** mm.

HIGH CONCEPT

High concept ideas usually have a conceptual premise and narrative that can be reduced to a catchy phrase or striking image. This film and television term has become the basis for campaigns keyed to a wave of related project merchandising. Examples of high concept animated films are The Little Mermaid and Aladdin.

IN-BETWEENING

In-betweening refers to the transitional motions between two extreme points of an animated character performing an action or an object in motion. The in-betweening function creates a series of frames in which the character or object makes incremental moves between the first key frame and the subsequent action in the next key frame.

116

LIP-SYNC

In animation, lip-sync is the simultaneity of a character's dialogue on the sound track and lip movement of the image.

LIVE-ACTION

Live-action refers to events in a film performed by living people as distinguished from those performed by animated figures.

MIXING

Mixing is the process of combining the individual sound tracks for dialogue, music and sound effects onto a single composite sound track. This process is usually accomplished in a theatre or studio where the film is projected onto a screen with a footage counter beneath.

MODEL SHEET

A model sheet, in animation, refers to a source in which a particular character or object is visually analyzed in various positions and angles to which all drawings conform.

MORPHING

Morphing is a computer-generated special effect that portrays one shape or form seamlessly changing into an entirely different shape or form.

MOUSE

A mouse refers to a data command device that supplements or replaces the keyboard. First, it was used as a pointer in paint programs and other graphic applications by transferring data into a form that is recognizable to the computer. Other command devices include keyboards, voice recognition and virtual reality gloves.

MOVIOLA

Moviola is the trade name of a portable motor-driven film-viewing machine that is upright or table variety, with the latter replacing the former. A Moviola is often used to synchronize animation tracks and for editing. Although there are numerous flatbed editing units manufactured by various companies, they are still referred to as Moviolas.

OPAQUER

In the early stages of animation production, opaquers flipped cels over and painted in the colors of the characters. This process is now accomplished by computers.

PEG

A peg is a standard screw-in protuberance on an animator's drawing board to accommodate Oxberry or Acme registration, over which pre-punched paper or cels are held in place. A peg bar is usually part of the animator's disk.

PENCIL TEST

A pencil test is a film or video sample of preliminary action and animation, drawn on paper, before it is converted to cel by computer.

POINT OF VIEW or POV

The term normally applies to the eyes through which we view the action. In animated films, the dominant perspective belongs to the neutral camera, although there are frequent divergences from this perspective to those of various characters.

MUSIC SPOTTING

Music spotting determines the location of animation music, dialogue and sounds on the sound track. Those decisions are usually made by the director at a Moviola or screening room with the composer, editor and sound effects editor.

STOP-MOTION

Stop-motion refers to a single-frame cinematic technique that utilizes the constant stopping and starting of the camera to allow for a change in the subject during the interval that the camera is not shooting. The action will appear to flow smoothly when the final film is projected.

STORYBOARDING

Storyboarding refers to the act of creating a storyboard, which is the visual system for making a detailed analysis of the film's development, including character appearance and movement, detailed sketches of backgrounds, delineation of scenes and sequences, and notes regarding music and sound effects.

TIMING

Timing is the process of altering the density and color values of a film from shot to shot or scene to scene during printing, in order to achieve consistency, balance or some effect. These decisions are made in the laboratory by the director, timer and cameraman.

TRANSFER

The term transfer is used when one copies the picture or sound being transmitted by one recorder onto another, or makes a videotape copy from film.

STUDIES OFFERED IN ANIMATION AND COMPUTER GRAPHICS

Each of the following school entries includes the name, address and phone number of the institution, describing its size, location and school calendar. In addition to indicating relevant degrees offered, information is provided concerning curricular emphasis and production facilities.

As a sampling of what this country has to offer regarding animation studies, the list generally provides information on formal university study, although several programs for the working adult or those making a career transition are included. I have selected schools that offer traditional studies geared toward a career in the animation industry as well as those institutions favoring an independent arts approach.

Although not listed here, more and more community colleges are offering courses in computer graphics, basic animation and video production studies. Usually, one must register early to be assured of a place, but most schools provide an accessible and affordable introduction to the craft of computer graphics as well as cel animation.

The POV that concludes each school listing is borrowed from the term *point of view* and provides a summary of each school's offerings and approaches.

A final note: Inasmuch as agendas, schedules and programs are subject to change, students are urged to contact individual schools regarding up-to-date information.

121

CALIFORNIA

CALIFORNIA COLLEGE OF ARTS AND CRAFTS
5275 Broadway, Oakland, CA 94618-1487
(510)653-8118.

Private professional arts college. Coed, urban location. Undergraduate enrollment: 1,100. Graduate enrollment: 70.

Calendar: Semesters.
Degrees Offered: B.F.A., M.F.A.

Curricular Emphasis: Film/Video/Performance. An animation workshop covers the basics of film animation and its applications to video and computer graphics. Focus is given to teaching the fundamentals of cel animation in conjunction with other methods such as claymation, while exploring both commercial and fine arts applications. The course entitled Computer Mediated Postproduction and Image Creation examine the use of computer-based tools to coordinate and control multiple tracks of sound, image and visual effects, including basics of 3-D modeling and animation.

Facilities/Equipment: The Computer Center makes available multiple Macintoshes with Premiere, Quark, Director and Photoshop software and NewTek Video Toasters. A separate lab contains a J/K Animation Stand with Thing M controller. Also on hand is a J/K dual optical printer with Thing M Controller, a NewTek Video Toaster in a multi-format editing suite and a Rutt Etra video synthesizer. A Sandine Image Processor, both four track and eight track analog audio recorders as well as Macintosh with a Protools digital audio system are also available.

POV: This small selective arts college offers animation training in the context of an experimental film and video production program as well as studies in computer-aided design.

CALIFORNIA INSTITUTE OF THE ARTS
McBean Pkwy., Valencia, CA 91355
(805)253-7825

Private comprehensive arts institution. Coed, suburban location. Undergraduate enrollment: 700. Graduate enrollment: 350.

Calendar: Semesters.
Degrees Offered: B.F.A., M.F.A., Film/Video, B.F.A., M.F.A., Art. Animation Program. There is a concentration in character animation at Cal Arts, with a core curriculum including Life Drawing; Character Design; Character Animation; Basic Color and Design; Layout; Story Development.

Experimental Animation Program. Courses include Computer Graphics; Animation Sketchbook; Computer Animation and Music/Iris-Wavefront; Advanced Computer Graphics/Video Studio; Motion Control; Oxberry Camera Operation; Optical Printer Operation; Direct Animation.

Art Department. Both the Art and Graphic Design programs offer the courses Advanced Digital Synthesis and Motion Graphics.

Facilities/Equipment: Students in animation programs use Amiga and Iris-Wavefront computers, a motion control camera and a computerized optical printer as well as computer controlled animation stands. There are video studios using a CMX video-editing computer as well as several cuts-only editing bays able to mix digital and analog video. A video synthesizer and MIDI are available. Students may also use the Center for Experiments in Art, Information and Technology and those studying computer graphics design may utilize two computer animation laboratories with eight Mac SE's, two SE/30's, two color IIs and a IIcis and two Laser Writers IIntx. There is also image scanning and both black and white as well as color video digitizing equipment.

123

POV: Founded in 1961 by Walt Disney, Cal Arts offers separate, complete degree programs in character animation and experimental animation through its state-of-the-art School of Video and Film. Computer graphics training is also available through the School of Art, the Music Department and the Critical Studies Department, with strong emphasis on the production of innovative works.

SAN FRANCISCO ART INSTITUTE
Chestnut St., San Francisco, CA 94133
(415)771-7020

Private arts institution. Coed, urban location. Undergraduate enrollment: 578. Graduate enrollment: 250.

Calendar: Semesters.
Degrees Offered: B.F.A., M.F.A., Filmmaking, B.F.A., M.F.A., Performance/Video.

Curricular Emphasis: Filmmaking is taught in a fine arts context, where the intent of the maker is primary. The intermedia courses offered combine film and other art disciplines. Studio courses in video explore video sculpture, narrative video, teleperformance, installation, computer-based interactive forms based on virtual reality, screen-mediated images, site-sensitive approaches related to architecture and other approaches. There are technical workshops.

Facilities/Equipment: Students have access to two animation stands, one with a tracking camera mount and rotoscope capabilities. There are two pin-registration optical printers. The computer arts facility houses a variety of equipment. Complete video production and post-production facilities are available.

POV: Established in 1871, the San Francisco Art Institute is one of the oldest schools of art in America, with a highly selective, professionally-equipped Fine Arts program for filmmakers and video artists.

This supportive artist-based community has 24-hour access to facilities and utilizes a faculty consisting of practicing media artists.

UNIVERSITY OF CALIFORNIA AT LOS ANGELES
405 Hilgard Ave., Los Angeles, CA 90024
(310)825-4321

Research university. Coed, urban location. Undergraduate enrollment: 23,000. Graduate enrollment: 12,000.

Calendar: Quarters.
Degrees Offered: B.A. in Film and Television, M.F.A. in Animation.

Curricular Emphasis: There is an undergraduate emphasis and a graduate major available in animation through the Animation Workshop, with projects ranging from conceptual to narrative animation, cel to computer animation, entertainment to experimental animation and active to interactive animation, depending on the individual's choice of style and direction.

Facilities/Equipment: The animation studio includes three animation cranes, one of which is 16/35mm, a video pencil test unit, a computer pencil test unit and several microcomputers with 2-D paint animation, 3-D object animation and interactive programs. Two 16mm optical printers are available as are complete sound editing and viewing facilities. Complete film and video production and postproduction facilities are available. The extensive animation collection in the UCLA Film and Television Archive is supplemented by those in the Workshop's own archives.

POV: All works made in this selective program remain the property of the artists who created them. The animation workshop offers three undergraduate and seven graduate courses as well as graduate thesis courses. The abiding philosophy stresses individual creative control over all aspects of film. The program provides national and interna-

125

tional guest lecturers and there are animation internships through the Visual Arts program. The university also offers an extension program in computer graphics, giving special attention to computer animation and interactive multimedia. The UCLA Extension's Department of Entertainment Studies and Performing Arts offers certificates at two levels as well as training in graphics and cel animation.

UNIVERSITY OF SOUTHERN CALIFORNIA
University Park, Los Angeles, CA 90089-2111.
(213)740-2311

Private comprehensive institution. Coed, urban location. Undergraduate enrollment: 16,000. Graduate enrollment: 12,000.

Calendar: Semesters.
Degrees Offered: B.A., Film/Video Production, M.F.A., Film, Video and Computer Animation.

Curricular Emphasis: In the School of Cinema and Television, undergraduates may elect a variety of animation studies. The newly created production-intensive Graduate Program emphasizes originality in the exploration and mastery of animation. The curriculum's approach provides students with the opportunity to create artwork that integrates state-of-the-art computing with high-end film and video technology, including 35mm and 70mm Omnimax film recording. The curriculum covers classical character and experimental animation, encouraging projects that explore new forms, including interactive multimedia, performance and installation art, the combination of live-action and computer animation, scientific visualization and virtual reality. Both programs are augmented by offerings from the Production and Critical Studies Departments.

Facilities/Equipment: A Complete Film Animation Studio is available to students with two 5300 Oxberry animation stands, one Bowlds-Acme animation stand, a Producer's Service 104 optical printer and three single-frame, color video animation systems. The computer animation lab includes over twenty-five Silicon Graphics workstations including Crimsons, Reality Engines and Indigos with SoftImage, Alias, Wavefront, Renderman, Side Effects Prisms, Parallax and Pixibox software and an Apple Macintosh AV. The lab is networked to a 16 processor Silicon Graphics Power Challenge. There is a Solitaire Cine II Film Recorder. Full film, video and television production as well as postproduction is available, including AVID editing and a music scoring studio.

POV: This School of Cinema and Television was founded in 1929 to become the nation's first film school, offering professional undergraduate and graduate training for animators working in a wide spectrum. The new Graduate Animation Program integrates film and videomaking arts with the latest technologies of computer animation, multimedia and digital technologies. The innovative program enjoys support from Warner Bros., Hanna-Barbera Productions and Silicon Graphics. The department funds selected advanced projects. Entering classes in the graduate program are currently limited to twenty students. The Computer Animation Lab has produced animation for several IMAX films. SCFX, which is USC's special effects student organization, has been involved in various production projects.

FLORIDA

RINGLING SCHOOL OF ART AND DESIGN
Sarasota, FL 34234
(813)351-4614

Private professional arts institution. Coed, urban location.

Calendar: Semesters.
Degrees Offered: B.F.A., Computer Animation.

Curricular Emphasis: The Department of Computer Animation offers Art History; Traditional Animation I and II; Figure Drawing; Creative Geometry; Color and Design; Computer Animation I-IV; Drawing Techniques; Concept Development; Video Production; Storyboarding Techniques; Scripting on UNIX Workstations; Special Topics in Computer Animation; Senior Project and Computer Animation Portfolio.

Facilities/Equipment: The computer classroom facilities include 11 Amiga 2000 and 7 Amiga 1200 computers. The lab has a video-grabbing device for video input and an HP Paintjet color printer for image output. The IBM PC lab is equipped with 12 IBM PCs and four compatibles. The Power Mac lab has twenty-four seats of the Power 7100/66 computers. This lab is equipped with a flatbed scanner, a slide scanner, video grabbing capabilities and two laser printers. The Silicon Graphics Indigo Lab houses the high-end computer animation hardware and software, including 16 Silicon Graphics Indigo XC24 workstations and digital compositing and painting with a variety of software. A complete Video Production facility is available.

POV: This well-equipped program offers a full major in computer animation with special emphasis on working creatively with motion and light within a simulated three-dimensional environment. Emphasis is placed on acquiring skills in conceptual development and the use of drawing as a tool for communication. Graduates are employed in areas of television advertising, entertainment and the special effects fields as well as emerging areas such as medical imaging, courtroom reconstructions, scientific and architectural visualizations, the development of video games and so on.

UNIVERSITY OF CENTRAL FLORIDA
4000 Central Florida Blvd., Orlando, FL 23816
(407)823-2000

State comprehensive institution. Coed, urban location. Undergraduate enrollment: 21,000. Graduate enrollment: 3,000.

Calendar: Semesters.
Degrees Offered: B.A. in Communications.

Curricular Emphasis: In the motion picture division, students may select the animation track with sequential course listings and advanced workshops in both cel and computer animation.

Facilities/Equipment: Complete facilities for both cel and computer graphics animation are available, while the graphics lab includes PC, Amiga, Mac, SGIs, Alias, film and video equipment.

POV: Complete production training is available with state-of-the-art facilities in film, animation, television and video. Advanced studies in both cel and computer animation are offered with some production access to major film studio facilities in the area.

GEORGIA

SAVANNAH COLLEGE OF ART AND DESIGN
342 Bull St., Savannah, GA 31401-3146
(912)238-2400

Private comprehensive arts institution. Coed, urban location. Undergraduate enrollment: 1,700. Graduate enrollment: 300.

Calendar: Quarters.
Degrees Offered: B.F.A., M.F.A., Computer Art; B.F.A., M.F.A., Video Production.

Computer Art Major. Computer animation courses offer electronic painting, "C" programming, multimedia, video production and post-production, 3-D modeling and animation and the history and aesthetics of computer art.

Video Major. Training is offered in video art as well as production, including music video, narrative, interactive, documentary and sound design.

Facilities/Equipment: Computer Art majors use eight computer graphics labs with Mac, Amiga, PC and Silicon Graphics workstations, single-frame controllers, video recording and a traditional animation lab. Students electing the Video major are provided with a voice-over studio, video wall and gallery, a digital audio system, a Tascam MidiStudio, video toasters with rendering stations, studio and field DAT recorder, single-frame controllers, character generators, a chro-makey studio and a Panther Dolly.

POV: This quality fine arts college offers a full computer graphics program with a concentration in computer animation. Undergraduate students work on storyboarding, scripting and production of two and three-dimensional computer animations, transferring their work to videotape with audio and special effects. Graduate students continue to explore 3-D animation, write storylines and design interactive programs from their own database of textual and visual information.

ILLINOIS

COLUMBIA COLLEGE
600 S. Michigan Ave., Chicago, IL 60605-1996
(312)663-1600

Private comprehensive institution. Coed, urban location. Undergraduate enrollment: 6,500. Graduate enrollment: 350.

Calendar: Semesters.
Degrees Offered: B.A., M.A., M.F.A., Film and Video.

Film and Video Program. There is a concentration in animation with course listings that include Animation I-III; Film Techniques; Animation Storyboarding and Concept Development; Animation Camera Seminar; Computer Animation; Drawing for Animation I and II; Stop-Motion Animation Techniques; 3-D Animation; Special Projects.

Computer Graphics Program. Course listings include Computer Graphics and Video; Computer Graphics Experimental Imaging; Computer Graphics 3-D Modeling/Animation; Mac II: Motion Graphics.

Facilities/Equipment: The animation studio has three Oxberry cameras, one motorized Mauer camera, a Bolex reflex camera and complete film and video production and postproduction. The computer graphics lab includes Amiga 1000s and 2000s, Mac IIs Nu Vista, IBM AT clones TARGA 16, Lumena 16, a film recorder, a camcorder, color printers, Liquid Light Imprint, a video digitizer and Crystal 3-D. An image capture system is available as well as a Diaquest frame controller, Digi-View, HyperCard PixelPaint and a variety of other graphics systems and software.

POV: Students choosing the Film and Video major receive intensive production-oriented film animation training. In addition, a full undergraduate major in computer graphics emphasizes state-of-the-art animation technology.

SCHOOL OF THE ART INSTITUTE OF CHICAGO
37 S. Wabash Ave., Chicago, IL 60603-3103
(312)899-5219

Private comprehensive arts institution. Coed, urban location. Undergraduate enrollment: 1,890. Graduate enrollment: 460.

Calendar: Semesters.
Degrees Offered: B.F.A., M.F.A., B.A., M.A.

Filmmaking. Students in independent film production are offered several animation courses, including Animation; Drawing for Animation; 2-D Computer Animation.

Art and Technology. Course listings include Experimental Computer Imaging; Advanced Computer Imaging; Computer Graphics Programming; 2-D and 3-D Computer Animation; Interactive Media; Kinetics; Holography.

Video. Students explore image manipulation, multichannel installations, experimental, narrative and documentary forms while developing their personal style.

Facilities/Equipment: An Oxberry animation stand is available as well as an Oxberry 1500 optical printer, a video synthesis systems, a sound studio with complete film and video production and postproduction facilities with a color special effects generator, a character generator and specially designed equipment to support electronic experimentation. The computer graphics lab includes Macintosh II computers, Amiga 2000 computers, IBM and compatible computers with Lumena software and Silicon Graphics personal Iris computers with Alias software, various animation software, video digitizers, color scanners, color printers, film recorders and video recording equipment. There are keyboards with MIDI interfaces for digital recording. In addition, there are holography studios and an electronics workshop for building computer-controlled kinetic sculptures and interactive installations.

POV: The School of the Art Institute is a fine arts institution offering comprehensive studies in cel animation as well as documentary and experimental film and video production. In addition, there are quality studies in computer programming for animation, image processing and for the development of synthetic realities and virtual environments. Both multi-disciplinary arts interaction and the exploration of new technologies is strongly promoted. There are visiting video artists. The highly innovative interdisciplinary Time Arts Program promotes studies in art and technology by blending work in computer-aided art and design, video, filmmaking, electronics and kinetics, sound, lasers and performance.

NEW YORK

PRATT INSTITUTE
200 Willoughby Ave., Brooklyn, NY 11205
(718)636-3600

Private comprehensive institution. Coed, urban location. Undergraduate enrollment: 3,000. Graduate enrollment: 750.

Calendar: Semesters.
Degrees Offered: B.F.A., M.F.A., Computer Graphics. B.F.A., Media Arts.

Department of Computer Graphics and Interactive Multimedia. Undergraduate courses include Introduction to Computer Graphics I and II; Introduction to Computer Graphics Programming I and II; Graphic Design with a Computer I and II; 3-D Modeling with Computer Graphics I; Introduction to 3-D Computer Modeling and Animation; 3-D Computer Animation I and II; Interactive Media I; Computer-Aided Design and Drafting I and II; Computer Graphics Portfolio; Illustration with Computer Graphics; Computer Graphics In Context.

Graduate Program in Computer Graphics. Options in computer animation with advanced computer animation workshops; interactive systems and multimedia; experimental media; electronic pre-press.

Media Arts Department. Students work in both film and video with undergraduate course listings that include Animation; Film and Television Graphics; Computer Animation and Graphics for Film and Television; Postproduction Computer Animation as well as Graphics for Film and Television; Postproduction Computer Animation and Graphics; Video Graphics for the Artist and Designer; Advanced Postproduction.

Facilities/Equipment: The computer graphics resources include 35 Apple Macintosh and Quadra computers with graphics boards and color monitors, a large selection of graphics software including interactive multimedia, animation and electronic pre-press programs. Ten Silicon Graphics workstations run the Alias and SoftImage three-dimensional modeling and animation software. There is one Quantel Graphic Paintbox and fifteen PC-compatible computers have Targa graphics boards, graphics tablets as well as assorted input and output peripherals that run the Tips paint and image processing program. One Sony 3/4" Video Editing System has an A/B roll and special effects capabilities. There is a large array of input and output peripherals, including video recorders, film recorders, printers and scanners. Computer resources are available through other Pratt programs which include a DEC VAX 6210 minicomputer, three Skok CAD systems, ten Sun Sparc stations as well as dozens of additional PC and Macintosh systems.

POV: This highly-ranked, well-equipped art school offers twenty-four hour access to facilities. The program in Computer Graphics prepares students for careers in computer animation and video production as well as in design, publishing, software development and electronic and interactive databases. A master's program in computer graphics is available with advanced thesis projects. The Media Arts Department provides undergraduate studies in both cel and computer animation with special attention given to computer animation and graphics techniques for film and television. This curriculum combines photography, film, video and animation studies into one academic area in which students elect a specific field of concentration while acquiring experience in all facets of the department's program of studies.

SCHOOL OF VISUAL ARTS
209 E. 23rd St., New York, NY 10010
(212)592-2100

Private professional arts institution. Coed, urban location. Undergraduate enrollment: 2,750. Graduate enrollment: 320.

Calendar: Semesters.
Degrees Offered: B.F.A., Film, Video and Animation. B.F.A., M.F.A., Computer Art.

Film, Video and Animation Department. Students may receive training in directing; screenwriting; cinematography; editing; animation; video art; studio and field production with ENG. Course listings include Introduction to Film Animation; Animation Drawing I and II; Action Analysis and Timing; Camera and Editing; Special Effects; Puppet Animation; Animation Workshop I and II; Video Art; Video Image Processing; Animation Thesis.

Computer Art Department. Course listings include Computer Animation; Computer Graphics I, II and III; 3-D Animation; Computer Drawing; 3-D Modeling and Animation; Computer Design; MacGraphics; Film and Video with the Computer; Digital Photography; Desktop Animation; Scripts and Animation; Computers in Art; 3-D Illustration and Design; Image Making; workshops.

Facilities/Equipment: There are two Oxberry animation cameras, two pencil-test animation video systems, an optical bench for film and Moviola and Steenbeck editing machines with sound track analyzation equipment. A computer graphics lab houses IBM and Macintosh computers with Amiga, Easel, Dr. Halo, Deluxe Paint and a variety of other systems and software. Complete film, video and television production as well as postproduction facilities are available.

POV: Providing quality instruction for animators and computer graphics artists, this school, which started as an institution for cartooning and illustration, is now America's largest independent art school, offering a media program with sequential course listings in animation as well as hands-on training in both film and video production. Students have twenty-four hour access to equipment. A separate program exists in computer art and graphics which covers computer animation for film and video as well as a variety of other projects in computer graphics and design. Both undergraduate and graduate programs in computer graphics are offered. Programs maintain one to one student to computer ratio. There is a separate program in Illustration and Cartooning. Animation students are expected to complete a short thesis film in any animation technique, creating characters, design and sound tracks.

SYRACUSE UNIVERSITY
Syracuse, NY 13244
(315)443-1033

Private comprehensive institution. Coed, urban location. Undergraduate enrollment: 11,000. Graduate enrollment: 4,000.

Calendar: Semesters.
Degrees Offered: B.F.A., M.F.A., Art Media Studies.

Curricular Emphasis: A diverse curriculum includes courses in filmmaking, computer graphics, composition animation, photography, advanced video postproduction techniques, screenwriting, sound techniques and experimental production, along with requirements in film and video theory, history and criticism. Separate undergraduate filmmaking tracks are available either in film art or film drama. Students choosing the film art track may take a variety of studio art electives. Computer graphics listings include Introduction to Computer Graphics for the Visual Arts; Intermediate Computer

Graphics for the Visual Arts; Advanced Computer Graphics for the Visual Arts; Graduate Computer Graphics for the Visual Arts; separate concentration in Art Video.

Facilities/Equipment: A 16mm Oxberry animation studio, an optical printer studio and complete film and video production to postproduction facilities are available, including an Amiga toaster and special effects equipment for video. The computer graphics lab includes Macintosh II FX with Nu-Vista board and a VAX 8810 network, Sun workstations, Tek cluster, Silicon Graphics Iris, numerous PCs and a connection machine.

POV: The School of Art and Design of Syracuse University is one of the oldest and most highly-rated schools in America, offering students a curriculum in which freshmen explore twenty various programs of study before choosing a concentration. Both undergraduate and graduate programs exist in animation filmmaking, art video and computer graphics.

OREGON

NORTHWEST FILM CENTER
Portland Art Museum, 1219 SW Park Ave., Portland, OR 97205.
(503)221-1156

Regional media arts center. Coed, urban location. Undergraduate enrollment: 1,000.

Calendar: Two 15-week terms per academic year as well as a separate 10-week summer session.
Degrees Offered: B.F.A., Filmmaking and Animation, co-offered with the Pacific Northwest College of Art; Certificate Program in Film.

Curricular Emphasis: Hands-on production classes are available taught by professional filmmakers and videomakers. Sequential training is offered in film animation techniques. Three major film festivals are sponsored each year. There is a Residence Program featuring notable Filmmakers and Video Artists. Video art installations are publicly presented.

Facilities/Equipment: Animation stand; 16mm film and video production as well as postproduction facilities; digital sound design; digital video editing. Access is offered to a computer graphics lab through Pacific Northwest College of Art.

POV: Classes at this lively media arts center are primarily designed for the working professional who is either already active in film and video or wishing to make a career transition. Through affiliations with the Pacific Northwest College of Art and Maryhurst College, the Film Center offers accredited semester-long courses in filmmaking and animation toward earning a B.F.A. degree. The nondegree certificate program in film is a fourteen course sequence which culminates in the production of an original short film. Students may take up to four years to complete certificate requirements.

RHODE ISLAND

RHODE ISLAND SCHOOL OF DESIGN
Two College St., Providence, RI 02903-2791
(401)454-6100

Private professional arts institution. Coed, urban location. Undergraduate enrollment: 2,000. Graduate enrollment: 100.

Calendar: Semester plus winter session.
Degrees Offered: B.F.A., B.G.D.

Film, Animation and Video Program features a strong production-based curriculum for artists in cel and computer animation, film and video.

Graphic Design Program: A professional degree program in visual communication covers original design as it applies to film graphics, publications design, packaging and other areas.

Facilities/Equipment: Two Filmmaker and one Master Series animation stand are available to students. The IBM RS-6000 computer workstation runs Wavefront 3-D animation software. Also available are a variety of graphics systems and software, including a Mac Plus, Amigas, video digitizers, printers and plotters. Complete film and video production and postproduction facilities exist including an eight track mixing studio with MIDI/video/tape chase.

POV: A highly regarded fine arts college, the Rhode Island School of Design offers those undergraduate students gaining entrance into the Film, Animation and Video Program opportunities to work in both film and digital animation while refining conceptual and aesthetic skills. The program emphasizes individual authorship, craftsmanship and innovation in the time arts. Traditional drawing and design skills are counterbalanced with advanced technology. Subsequently, students must produce a finished work in order to graduate. The separate Graphics Design degree, instituted in 1989, was the first of its kind in American graphics design education. Various three to six week travel courses are also available.

INDEX

N

O

P

S

Ernest Pintoff

Academy Award® winning director for his animated short film called
The Critic. Ernest Pintoff lives in Hollywood with his wife, Caroline,
who is a pre-school teacher and artist.

THE INDEPENDENT FILM & VIDEOMAKER'S GUIDE
-2ND EDITION
Michael Wiese

Wiese has packed 25 years experience in film and video into the most comprehensive and most useful book ever for filmmakers seeking both independence and success in the marketplace. Loaded with insider's tips to help filmmakers avoid the pitfalls of show business, this book is the equivalent of a "street smart degree" in filmmaking.

This new, completely expanded and revised edition has all the information you need from raising the cash through distribution that caused the original edition to sell more than 35,000 copies.

Contents include writing mission statements, developing your ideas into concepts, scriptwriting, directing, producing, market research, the distribution markets (theatrical, home video, television, international), financing your film, pitching, presentations, writing a business plan, and a huge appendix filled with film cash flow projections, sample contracts, valuable contact addresses, and much more.

> *"A straightforward and clear overview on the business of making films or videos. Wiese covers the most important (and least taught) part of the job: creative deal-making. The book is full of practical tips on how to get a film or video project financed, produced, and distributed without sacrificing artistic integrity. A must for any aspiring independent producer."*
> **Co-Evolution Quarterly** (about the first edition)

$29.95, Approx. 500 pages, over 30 illustrations, 6 x 8 1/4, ISBN 0-941188-57-4, Order # 37RLS

On Sale
September 1998

To order this book for classroom use, please call Focal Press at 1-800-366-2665.

THE DIRECTOR'S JOURNEY
THE CREATIVE COLLABORATION BETWEEN DIRECTORS, WRITERS AND ACTORS
Mark W. Travis

What if you could be instructed, one-on-one with a top-notch directing coach who would help you develop your own directorial style?

Mark W. Travis takes the mystery out of directing. His refreshing approach will enhance and broaden your directing skills and help you deliver powerful performances and well-conceived cohesive films.

Contents include material on the script, script breakdown, assembling the team, casting, rehearsing, production and postproduction.

This long-awaited book is based on the methods Travis has developed in his popular directing seminars, which have been attended by hundreds of film directors in Los Angeles, New York, and Japan.

MARK W. TRAVIS has directed over 50 plays, many hours of episodic television, and the Warner Brothers' feature film, *Going Under*.

"A comprehensive and inspired examination of craft. A must-read for any serious professional."
Mark Rydell, Director,
On Golden Pond, The Rose

"With an astonishing clarity Mark Travis articulates the techniques and skills of film directing."
John Badham, Director,
Saturday Night Fever, War Games, Blue Thunder

The #1 Best Selling Non-Fiction Paperback, Los Angeles Times,
September 1997
A Doubleday Stage & Screen Book Club Selection

$26.95, 350 pages, 6 x 8-1/2, ISBN 0-941188-59-0, Order # 29RLS

FILM DIRECTING
SHOT BY SHOT
Steven Katz

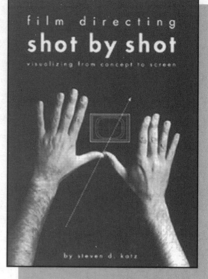

Every page in this international best-seller is loaded with career-saving information for both first-time directors and seasoned pros. It is filled with visual techniques for filmmakers to expand their stylistic knowledge. With beautiful illustrations and expertly written directions, *Shot by Shot* has been used as a reference tool "on the set" by many of Hollywood's directors.

Provides insight into the work of Spielberg, Welles and Hitchcock with many **never before published** storyboards for *Empire of the Sun, Citizen Kane, The Birds.* If you read no other film book, read this one!

"...helps (students) move the film that's in their head to paper and communicate it to their actors and crew..."

Professor Fred Watkins, University of North Texas
Department of Radio TV Film, Denton, Texas

"...an excellent text for teaching students how to visualize the flow of shots in a scene and how to incorporate storyboards into preproduction."

Professor Duane Meeks, Regent University
School of Cinema Television

A Doubleday Stage & Screen Book Club Selection

$24.95, 370 pages, 7 x 10, 750+ illus.
ISBN: 0-941188-10-8
Order # 7RLS

FILM DIRECTING
CINEMATIC MOTION
Steven Katz

Learn how to stage and block those tricky scenes. This idea-packed book includes discussions of scheduling, staging without dialogue, staging in confined spaces, actor and camera choreography in both large and small spaces, sequence shots, and much more. Learn the production requirements from a well-known cinematographer, director, production manager, continuity person, and actor as they discuss approaches to camera space and movement. This book will clear up anxieties on your very next shoot.

$24.95, ISBN 0-941188-14-0, 200 pages, 7 x 10, over 400 illustrations
Order # 6RLS

PRODUCER TO PRODUCER
INSIDER TIPS FOR ENTERTAINMENT MEDIA - 2ND EDITION
Michael Wiese

Here's a wide range of insightful advice on creative techniques that will save and earn you thousands of dollars when producing, financing, or marketing.

Twenty-one new chapters on independent producing, home studios, starting out, directing, network specials, direct-to-video movies, legal issues, creating hit videos and much more are here for you to use today.

MICHAEL WIESE is a producer and director with more than 25 years experience in film, television, pay TV, and home video. He has presented independent film seminars in Europe, Australia, Indonesia, and throughout the United States.

$24.95, 350 pages, 6 x 8-1/4
ISBN 0-941188-61-2
Order # 28RLS

THE INDEPENDENT FILM

MICHAEL WIESE PRODUCTIONS
11288 Ventura Blvd., Suite 821
Studio City, CA 91604
1-818-379-8799
kenlee@earthlink.net
www.mwp.com

Write or Fax
for a
free catalog.

Please send me the following
books:

Title   Order Number (#RLS___)   Amount

_____   _____

_____   _____

_____   _____

_____   _____

SHIPPING   _____

California Tax (8.25%)   _____

TOTAL ENCLOSED   _____

Please make check or money order payable to
Michael Wiese Productions

(Check one) ____ Master Card ____Visa ____Amex

Credit Card N

Expiration Dat

Cardholder's

Cardholder's

SHIP TO:

Name____

Address____

City____

HOW TO ORDER
CALL
24 HOURS
7 DAYS A WEEK

CREDIT CARD
ORDERS
CALL
1-800-833-5738

OR ## FAX YOUR
ORDER
818-986-3408

OR ## MAIL THIS
FORM

SHIPPING
ALL ORDER MUST BE PREPAID
UPS GROUND SERVICE
ONE ITEM - $7.00
EACH ADDTLN ITEM, ADD $2

SPECIAL REPORTS - $2 EACH.
EXPRESS -3 BUSINESS DAYS
ADD $12 PER ORDER

OVERSEAS
SURFACE - $15.00 EACH ITEM
AIRMIAL - $30.00 EACH ITEM